I0116511

Traditional Publishing
Write a Great Novel, Book 5

by
G. R. Sixbury

**Traditional Publishing: Writing Fiction That Sells
(Write a Great Novel 5)**

Copyright © 2017 by G. R. Sixbury

Published by Kansix Books, Inc.

ISBN-13: 978-1-947317-05-5

ISBN-10: 1-947317-05-9

All Rights Reserved. No part of this publication may be reproduced, stored in a retrieval system, or transmitted in any form or by any means without the prior permission of the publisher.

Dedications

Thanks to all of my students. Hopefully I managed to teach you as much as you taught me.

Preface

Most of the writers I know fall into two camps: those who believe traditional-publishing is the only way to go and those who believe self-publishing is the only model that makes sense in our modern world.

This book is for those writers who want to have their work published under the tried-and-true traditional method. That is, they want to write their novel, sell that novel to someone else who will copyedit it, typeset it, and publish it. With luck, the folks who do the buying might even do some editing and marketing along the way. The finished product will show up in bookstores and maybe even libraries. More important, writers pursuing the traditional model will receive that validation that says a professional in the publishing field felt their work was so good that they went to bat for them, probably paid them in advance for their work, and brought their creation to market.

Table of Contents

Part I: The Chosen Path

That Way Is a Very Nice Way

For a moment, let's talk about the **easiest possible** road a writer can follow to publication.

First—and most important—let's assume you've spent your whole life preparing to write. That means reading, writing great essays for school, excelling at grammar and syntax, developing a great work ethic, finishing what you start, and struggling through some dark times and coming through them stronger than ever. Second, you have a great idea for a novel or a series of novels. This one is always given too much credit by beginning writers. Yes, a great idea is important, but the way you develop that idea is much more important. J. K. Rowling grossed a billion dollars off her Harry Potter series of novels, but in the hands of nearly any other writer, it would have seen little success. Third, you write the novel to the best of your ability. Fourth, just after you've finished the last polish on your manuscript, you're talking to your neighbor about this great novel you've written and she mentions that her editor cousin from New York is coming for dinner that night and why don't you come over, manuscript in hand? Fifth, you follow your neighbor's suggestion, hit it off with the editor who loves you, loves your manuscript, and has need of a book just like yours to fill a slot in her spring lineup. Within a week after returning to New York, you receive a contract and six-figure check. Sixth, a year later your novel comes out with a novel launch party backed by a million dollar marketing campaign. Seventh, you sit back raking in the dough from royalties and movie deals while you leisurely work on your next book.

Impossible? It would be a bit like winning the giant Powerball lottery, but people do that every year. It's not impossible to win the lottery, no matter what my Statistics professor claimed. It's also not impossible to live the scenario painted above, but it is *incredibly unlikely*. However, it is by far the easiest and quickest road to publication.

That's why I bring it up. If you want the chance to make the most money with the least amount of work on your part, you need to attempt to sell your novel to a traditional publishing house. Understand that when I say the least amount of work, that doesn't mean that it's a small amount. You still need to write a great novel, you still have marketing to do, cover blurbs to write, interviews to arrange and give, readers and editors to charm, and all the rest. But traditional publishing provides the most help that you can get.

Write First, Sell Later

When I teach my writing classes, everyone always wants to know how to sell their novel. They sit enraptured as I talk about agents and contracts and book signings. They ask detailed questions about whether they need an agent and which publishers would be likely to buy their work.

But they haven't written a word.

There is one absolute universal truth when it comes to writing. You never get a second chance to make a good first impression. Whoever reads your novel, whether it be editor, agent, or glorious reader, they will judge your novel based on what you've written. Granted, they might be predisposed to like it or hate it based on circumstances, but a lousy novel can repel the most eager reader and a great novel can ensnare the most reluctant one.

Nearly all of the information provided in this book is only useful after you've finished your book. (For more information about writing your novel, feel free to consult the many sources available, including other books available in the Write a Great Novel series.)

When you start looking for a market for your novel, that novel should be as finished and as ready to print as you ever plan to make it. If you're not comfortable with the novel you've written going straight to press, it's not done yet. Finish it first, then find someone to buy it. I've actually had wanna-be writers tell me that they needed to sell the novel they were working on so that their editor could help them finish it.

If you're a movie star who just had sex with the president and you plan to write a tell-all book, selling your book first will actually work. But if you're writing a novel, not only should you finish the novel before you try to sell it, but also you should strive to make it as good as you can make it before you let anyone read it.

By anyone, I'm talking about anyone outside friends and family and writing groups. Even for those folks, you should provide a review copy that's the best you can create. Nothing is more self-centered than asking other people to critique a manuscript containing problems that you know how to correct but didn't bother to fix before you asked them to tell you what you already knew.

Traditional Publishing: What You Get

A respected, long-time chief editor at a major publisher house once told me, "An editor's job is not to buy novels from authors. An editor's job is to sell the novels they've already bought."

This point is often lost on beginning writers. An editor's job is not to discover unknown writers or help those writers publish a successful novel. Editors aren't there to be your friends; they provide one part of a business transaction. Chances are they won't fix your novel, give great advice, or improve your book in any way. What they will do is try to sell your novel after they've purchased it. The amount of effort they expend selling your novel depends directly on how much they paid for that novel. If they gave you a million dollar advance, your novel will receive the red carpet treatment. If they paid you the minimum advance they ever give out, you will receive the lowest level of service.

Guess which of those two groups most beginning writers fit into. Hint: It's not the million dollar advance group.

So what services can you expect to receive from a traditional publishing house? In essence, why should you go the traditional route rather than just publishing the novel yourself?

Pros and Cons of Traditional Publishing

You bought this book, so obviously you're interested in traditional-publishing. Why read about the pros and cons of your decision? The choice is already made, right?

Not necessarily.

Unless you've already sold a couple novels to a big New York publishing house, you probably haven't encountered much of what you need to know to be successful. Even if you know that traditional publishing is the only kind of publishing you would ever consider, you can use this section as validation for your decision. Better yet, use it when you're helping your writer friends decide on the best publishing model for their work.

Below I've broken out the advantages and disadvantages of traditional publishing. Use the list below to determine whether your best course of action is to try to publish your novel through the traditional model or whether you would be better served publishing your book yourself.

<u>Advantages</u>

- Limited workload after novel is complete:
    1) Correct your manuscript based on editing and copy editing feedback
    2) Create basic marketing materials, such as suggestions for cover, back cover blurb, tag lines, 1-3 paragraph marketing synopsis, selling points, expected market, current competition to your novel, etc.
    3) Fill out a new author questionnaire
    4) Solicit blurbs from other authors recommending your novel
    5) Provide head shot for publicity photos
    6) Set up signings, interviews, news releases, and most other forms of publicity
- No need to create or hire someone to
    1) Create cover art
    2) Typeset the novel
    3) Copy edit the novel

- Presence in brick and mortar bookstores and in school and public libraries
- Better visibility on electronic book sites
- You get paid an advance before publication

Disadvantages

- You still need to do all the work listed under the advantages. Further disadvantages:
  1) Limited control regarding what changes to your novel you accept
  2) Little to no control over any of the marketing
  3) Complete blame if the novel fails to make back its advance
- No guarantee you will ever be published
- Limited royalties *after* earning out your advance, typically limited to 8-15% of retail price for printed novels and 25% for electronic novels (compared to self-publishing where you often receive 25% for printed and up to 35-70% for electronic)
- Your printed novels are remaindered after a ridiculously short time
- Impractically long consideration and publication time for first novels, often lasting years

Analysis

If you put a hundred writers in a room, you'd get ninety-four different opinions on pretty much any subject. When it comes to traditional vs. self-publishing, we might have to jump that to ninety-nine out of one hundred. I can only imagine the pushback you'd get from this chart if you showed it to either editors at traditional publishing houses or to successful self-published authors. One fact is certain: Neither model works for everyone.

Based on my own personal perspective, traditional publishing provides one real and consistent advantage: Big houses have the ability to get your books in front of readers in a way that a lone, beginning writer simply can't match. In decades past, their ability to get your novel in a brick and mortar store was huge. In today's world, those stores are vanishing. If you're writing a YA novel or a children's book, the ability to get that book on the shelves of libraries across the country is still a huge advantage. It's no surprise that there are few successful self-published children's authors. But even if we throw out the physical presence on bookshelves, large publishers have a distinct advantage and preferential treatment when it comes to the novels they offer on sites like Amazon. All beginning writers face a serious uphill battle getting their first novels noticed in the marketplace.

As a result, if you are a writer who can't achieve a high level of production (meaning you—at best—write a novel every year or two), traditional publishing might be your best bet. Provided your novel sells well enough, traditional publishers can support you while you gradually build up your readership through years of effort. This doesn't mean you can write a novel once a decade and have high hopes for success, but publishers have clout to get your novel in front of readers even without frequent production on your part. That's nearly impossible as a self-published author.

Students often ask what I mean by frequent production. I know self-published writers who turn out four novels a month. Literally. And that's not for just one particular month. That's month after month after month. Other self-published authors have defiantly proclaimed that they aren't particularly productive and only finish three to four novels a year. If even these reduced productivity numbers seem downright scary to you, remember that these are professional authors. Their day job is their writing. But understand that writing quickly while writing well is a huge career advantage for a self-published author. It's pretty handy for a traditionally published author, also, but this multiple novel per year pace isn't as much of a requirement. I know plenty of successful traditionally published authors who finish one novel per year. If your pace is slower than that, then you better hope for wild success with your first novel.

From my perspective the largest negative in traditional publishing is that it can take years to get a response from a publisher on a novel you've sent them for consideration. During that time, you're not allowed to send that novel to anyone else. It's an inconceivably flawed system that effectively discourages and blocks new writers from publication. Many argue it's necessary, but it's still elitist and wrong—and incredibly prone to mistakes.

The only reliable method to avoiding waiting years just to be told no is to short-circuit the system by finding an agent or by making a personal connection to an editor. I would argue that if you have the marketing savvy to do that, you have a good deal of what it takes to be a successful self-publishing novelist. If you can market yourself to an agent or an editor, you can market your own novel directly to your readers. But what if you want to buy that lottery ticket that the big publishing houses are offering? In that case, you're going to want an agent—or at the very least, you're going to want to bypass the slush pile wall blocking access to the editor's desk. We cover what you need to know about agents in the "Literary Agents" section, but before you go looking for an agent, you need to make sure your book has the best chance for success once it reaches the editor's desk.

There is too much. Let me sum up

Traditional Publishing is the tried and true method of getting rich and famous that's been followed by most writers throughout recorded history. There's an excellent chance that traditional publishing in some form will still be around for centuries to come. To succeed under the traditional publishing model, you must rise above the competition.

- Traditional publishing is still the most reliable route to widespread fame and fortune, although your odds of winning the lottery aren't that much worse than becoming a best-selling author by selling your first novel.
- You should write, finish, and polish your novel before trying to sell it.
- Traditional Publishing is best suited for people who 1) are already famous, 2) can't produce the multiple novels per year self-publishing demands for success, or 3) are unwilling to learn or do the tasks performed by traditional publishers, such as cover blurbs, copy editing, cover art, and typesetting.

Part II: Your First Reader

A Different Kind of Audience

Editors and agents read manuscripts as one of their tasks at work. While both groups spend a good share of their time trying to sell the books they've already bought (or agreed to represent), both groups need to find new writers on occasion. They have no shortage of folks lining up to be considered for this honor. As a result, the time they have to spend on any given manuscript is limited.

Because they're professional readers, they read manuscripts differently than most people who read for pleasure. The biggest consequence of reading professionally versus for pleasure is that professionals develop shortcuts to save time. As a wanna-be writer, you need to be aware of these shortcuts and either embrace them or avoid them, as appropriate. Also, never consider a rejection by a professional editor or agent as a definitive reflection on what you've written. Professionals reject manuscripts for many reasons, only some of which are related to the quality of what you've written.

The Crap Sandwich

For those with delicate sensibilities, you might be offended by the word *crap*. If so, take your ball point, scratch out crap, and write poo. Mike Rowe would be proud.

When I was attempting (and failing) to sell my first novel, I grew curious about why my novel couldn't make it out of the slush pile. I'd read hundreds of novels in my life. Being as objective as possible, the overall quality of my novel was certainly not at the top of the heap compared to those published novels, but it wasn't dragging the murky bottom either. Why didn't editors send me a contract?

To solve the problem, I started reading first-novels. While it's always unclear whether the first novel an author sold is the first novel that author wrote, it's hard to argue that a relatively unknown author sold a manuscript. Why did the sale happen? By reading first-novels, I tried to determine if they shared any qualities in common.

That's when I discovered the crap sandwich.

Getting back to my experiment, what I found was that most first-novels had great beginnings and great endings but were laden with crap in the middle. While I would never encourage any writer to be satisfied with a less than stellar middle to his novel, I do claim that it's nearly impossible to sell a first-novel in today's marketplace without having a great beginning and a great ending unless you're famous or have some kind of personal and intimate connection to the editor, and even then, it's unlikely. Without putting your body on the market, especially if your body isn't trading so well against the yen, you have to have a great beginning and ending. You can (and most first-time novelists do) make mistakes in the middle. But the beginning and the ending of your novel must stand above and beyond the competition or your novel will probably fail.

Because beginnings and endings are so important, one of the books in the Write a Great Novel series is devoted entirely to that topic. As you might expect, it's called *Beginning to End*.

I mention the crap sandwich, because it represents the minimum requirement you must meet if you want to sell your work to a traditional market. Even if you have a great beginning and a great ending and a fairly fantastic middle, there are plenty of obstacles left to trip you up.

The Slush Party

Close your eyes. No, wait, don't close your eyes. Then you couldn't read this. Okay, imagine that you've closed your eyes. And then imagine the flood of unsolicited manuscripts that form massive slow-moving, ever-growing glaciers in most editorial offices. For most editors, these horrific piles of paper represent a necessary evil called the slush pile. (Granted, many editors have switched to electronic submissions. But a growing mountainous glacier of electrons isn't nearly as picturesque as that growing mass of paper.) This slush pile must be dealt with before its gradual growth consumes everything in sight. A small handful of editors have claimed they enjoy reading manuscripts from the slush pile. The fact they've since been taken away by men in white coats so they can get some much needed rest is a clear indication of their depleted mental state. Most normal editors, if you get a few drinks in them and they're sure they aren't being recorded, will admit that they dread diving into the slush pile. It's a task they delegate to underlings whenever possible. Like anyone else, they relish the anticipation that accompanies picking up a book they want to read. It's almost impossible to get that anticipation with a slush pile manuscript.

Going back to your imagination and those manuscript glaciers, let's pretend you're the editor. What's to be done? You hate the idea of reading them, but you and your team of assistant editors need to reach the copier and the piles of manuscripts are blocking your way. What now?

Slush party!

A slush party is a gathering of editors, assistant editors, and first readers who thresh their way through the slush pile and get rid of the chaff. Slush parties are often held on Friday nights. Pizza and drinks might be involved. The exact setup varies, but the goal remains the same:

> Legitimately reject as many manuscripts
> as possible in the shortest time possible.

This may seem harsh, but imagine you're one of these editors. You're underpaid. You're tired. You've been working hard all week, and your attendance at this slush party is a sacrifice of your personal time. Your grass hasn't been mowed, your spouse hasn't been kissed, you barely know your kids, and your dog growls and attacks whenever you come home because you're less familiar than the pizza delivery guy (and you're not carrying pizza). You have better things to do than attend a slush party.

Keeping you in check is the knowledge that you're not allowed to reject manuscripts without a reason. No one wants the job insecurity that comes from rejecting the next *Harry Potter* series. At the same time, as soon as you find a legitimate reason to reject a manuscript (the CYA principle applies here), your work on that item is done. Reach for the rejection letter, add their name to the email rejection list, or send up smoke signals. Regardless of how you get the word out, or whether you bother to inform the writer at all, that writer's time in the inner circle is done and you can move on.

I've heard that sometimes prizes are offered to the assistant who gets through the most manuscripts for the evening. Only the people at the parties know what really goes on. It should also be pointed out that each publishing house works differently and that this entire slush party concept is just in our imaginations. But one fact is irrefutable. Editors receive more manuscripts than they can buy. For big houses, they reject thousands of manuscripts every month. I've had editors claim they carefully read 10,000 short-story manuscripts per month. Sure. And I can fly provided no one's looking. What's certain is that some places reject 10,000 manuscripts per month, and those decisions have to happen somehow.

This may seem depressing. It's not meant to be. On the contrary, when that many manuscripts are rejected in such a short time and with such a small amount of consideration, you know several facts that should brighten your outlook: 1) When a novel you've sent into one of the big houses get's rejected, they aren't rejecting you or even any part of you, and 2) In most cases, they aren't even rejecting your manuscript, but rather are rejecting a small part of it that might have no bearing on your eventual readers. I'm not faulting the editors and first readers here. You try painting the *Mona Lisa* in six minutes flat and see how well you do. That's why most editors and first readers have developed handy flags and shortcuts that are reasonably reliable in predicting whether a manuscript will be publishable.

Regardless how the rejections get passed out, it's important to understand that your manuscript faces an uphill battle to reach publication and it's wise to give it the best chance you possibly can.

Editors Have Big Stones

Your chance of getting published is like an empty red wagon. You know, it's like those Radio Flyer® wagons kids used to pull around before the invention of handheld devices and the internet. Imagine you're a kid and you have one of those red wagons. You need to pull that wagon up a steep hill. Unlike Sisyphus from Greek mythology, it may be hard to get your wagon to the top of the hill, but it's not impossible. If you conquer the hill, you get published. Now picture that little red wagon filled with heavy stones to the point the axles are about to break. Suddenly the myth of Sisyphus is looking like a better analogy. You have no chance to ever get up and over that hill. Wouldn't it be nice to have that empty wagon back?

The nature of your book and how it's written determines the number and size of stones that get placed in that wagon. For the particular novel you're writing, you might have to put in a few stones because it wouldn't be your novel if you left them out. Even so, your goal as a beginning writer should be to keep that wagon as empty as possible. To that end, let's take a look at some of the obstacles that stand between you and publication.

Every editor (and every reader) is different. As writers, this makes our jobs more difficult. Even worse, both editors and professional writers often spout publishing absolutes. Do this; don't do that; always begin your novel, "It was a dark and stormy night...." Never begin your novel, "It was a dark and stormy night...." Sometimes they even have the audacity to suggest you should avoid prologues completely.

As a writer, it's futile to guess what a particular editor may or may not like, but some dislikes are so common that that they're worth your attention. If you recognize the stones that you're placing in your wagon, you can make an informed decision about whether the power of your story and your characters is strong enough to get your Radio Flyer® up that hill. I give this advice knowing many writers will reject it. For the ones who willingly overload their wagons, this advice will seem more plausible after they've made seventeen failed attempts to lug those stones up the publishing hill. It might convince them to throw a few stones out during a rewrite or at least help them avoid stacking so many stones in their wagon when they write their next novel.

To carry this analogy entirely too far, I've divided the possible stones you might add to your wagon into boulders and rocks. Stick a boulder in your wagon and you better strap a rocket to its belly if you want to get it up the hill. Rocks are easier to move, but too many together will almost always cause you to fail.

Boulders	Rocks
Bad manuscript formatting	Novel is mismatched for the house or the editor
Language mistakes	Prologues
Unsympathetic characters	Present tense
Irrelevant story	Not enough dialog in first few pages
Clichéd story	Not enough action in first few pages

Let's go through each of these briefly.

Boulders

As a general rule, boulders are usually impossible to haul up the hill. Avoid them whenever possible.

Bad manuscript formatting

For proper manuscript formatting, visit the publisher's web site and look for their Submission Guidelines. If you're sending your manuscript to an agent rather than a publishing house, they have submission guidelines, too. Write, call, email, check web sites; do whatever it takes to find out the proper format for your manuscript and use it. Almost all editors and agents consider bad manuscript formatting to be one of those unforgiveable curses. Fail to format your manuscript properly and it'll never be read.

Language Mistakes

This is one of those catch-alls to say that if you want to be a writer, know how to write correctly and well. You should study multiple books on grammar, style, and punctuation until you become an English language expert. Keep language reference materials handy when you rewrite. Also, understand that to be a successful writer, you need to be more than just a grammarian. You need proper syntax (putting together words in the proper order), correct semantics (using words that express the meaning you're trying to convey), and excellent diction (choice of words or style). An editor once told me that all problems with a novel are fixable if the story's good enough, *except* poor diction. Diction forms the underlying molecules from which a novel is constructed. Get that chemistry wrong and nothing can be done beyond rewriting the novel from scratch. Bad diction turns your novel into toxic waste.

Unsympathetic Characters

The sympathy here is on the part of the reader, not the characters. If you have unsympathetic characters, it means the reader doesn't care what happens to them. Usually characters are sympathetic when the reader can easily identify with them. This means it's easy for the reader to understand the characters' goals, problems, and feelings. It's why most fifty-year-olds have such difficulty reading teen angst fiction, why most guys avoid classic romance novels, and why most civilian women have no interest in military fiction. These are generalizations, but if you plan to write fiction, you need to understand the types of characters your audience expects and likes. If your novel's populated with unsympathetic characters, you've just heaved a huge stone into your wagon.

Irrelevant Story

Some story topics are naturally relevant: the entire world in peril, the love interest in a romance novel, the paranormal dangers in a horror novel, the murder in a mystery novel, etc. Once we go beyond the naturally relevant stories, it's impossible to define what's relevant and what isn't just by the topic. Instead, irrelevant stories are most easily identified by their irrelevance to the main character. If the story isn't all-encompassing for the main character, it's going to be difficult to create a relevant story for your readers. As a test, examine your main character. If you can replace him with another, significantly different character and the resulting story's the same, you've probably got an irrelevant story. That, or you've just written a 1950's science-fiction novel.

Clichéd Story

Clichéd stories are absolutely impossible to define, because it's always in the eye of the beholder. (In this case, the eye of the agent or editor.) A student of mine who we'll call Jake (because that was his name) once wrote a short story where a paleontologist discovered dinosaur bones on page one. The discovery was vital to Jake's story, but beyond that discovery, nothing relating to dinosaurs appeared again. Jake received a rejection letter that explained the editor was sick of dinosaur stories. What this proves is that editors see clichés where they don't exist, and Jake shouldn't have started his story at the dinosaur dig. Since Jake had no way to know that, the only valid way to avoid creating a clichéd story is to be intensely familiar with your market. If tons of stories or novels share the ideas or topics you express in your first few pages, you've knowingly loaded your wagon with a big stone. However, clichéd stories exist for a reason. Most people like those topics. That's why they're cliché. Vampire romances, anyone? The easiest way to change your boulder into a rock is to put a twist on the cliché. Have your vampires sparkle in sunlight instead of turning to dust, for example. The overall topic's still cliché, and therefore familiar, but it's also different and so becomes interesting. If you write that kind of story well enough, then you could have the next bestseller. Just be aware of the load you're placing in your wagon.

Novel is mismatched for the house or the editor

This one should be obvious. Do your research. Don't send stories or novels to editors or houses where they don't fit. By fit, I mean the market you send your manuscript to should publish the type of material you're sending. Don't submit Christian fiction to Playboy magazine's short story contest (or vice-versa). Don't send mystery novels to Microsoft Press. I'm giving blatant examples to make a point, but this stone is usually placed in the wagon when a genre writer sends out queries en mass to agents or sends short stories to every available market without checking out that market's guidelines. It also occurs quite often when writers ignore specific instructions. If an editor's accepting submissions for an anthology containing time-travel stories, don't send them a story where no one travels in time. Simply put, understand your markets. Find and read the guidelines. Send your manuscripts to markets where they have a chance to sell.

Rocks

It's common to have a couple rocks in your wagon. The ones listed here are some of the bigger ones. Having said that, if you have a need for one of these rocks, add it to your wagon. But be honest. If you haven't tried to write the novel without a prologue, for example, then you don't know if it can be done. Be most wary of adding any of these rocks to your wagon because you believe they will give you a *better* chance to sell your novel. They may be necessary, but they will almost always *decrease* the odds of selling your work versus having no rocks at all. Don't believe me? Then explain why the first Harry Potter novel was rejected so many times and why the first print run for the novel even after it was purchased was limited to only 500 copies. This is a novel that went on to sell many, many millions of copies in the bookstores. It had problems selling to editors because J. K. Rowling loaded her wagon with rocks, several of which appear in my list below.

Prologues

Some of you may still be seething over my recommendation to avoid prologues. While they're often a flag that signals "Amateur!" they do have a purpose. If the beginning of your book lays a great deal of groundwork without being particularly interesting or exciting, especially if there's information that can't be known by the main character in the early pages but must be known by the reader, prologues are sometimes necessary. Unfortunately, a prologue is usually written as an attempt to assure your readers that the book will get better. Beginning writers use this technique so often because they're smart enough to recognize that their beginnings are relatively boring, but not smart enough to realize that those beginnings should be fixed instead of throwing a prologue at the reader and hoping it blinds them long enough to sneak in your first three chapters. It's never a good idea to hold a carrot in front of the reader's nose like he's a donkey and expect him to lumber forward until you get to the good part. You never know when the reader will get tired of your little game and realize that what he's reading at that moment is boring. Editors are the least patient of readers. (See "The Slush Party".) If you must have a prologue because your novel simply won't work without it, then go ahead and add that stone to your wagon. But do so knowing how much it weighs.

Also, using flashbacks in your first couple chapters is nothing more than cutting that carrot into pieces before you offer it to the donkey. It's not fooling anybody. What gets you rejected here is starting your novel in the past when your story doesn't exist in the past. Feeding a reader an exciting, interesting, action-packed prologue (or flashback) and then forcing them to return to a mundane, uninteresting first chapter simply highlights why your book doesn't work. Skip the prologue (or flashback) and fix the real problem. Write an interesting first chapter that people want to read.

Present tense

Most writers dread being ordinary. Some inane editor or writer once told them that originality sells. Anyone who's watched the blockbuster movies coming out of Hollywood since the invention of "talkies" (and probably before) knows this isn't the case. Originality of method and originality of story idea aren't what sell. Originality of emotion is. You create originality of emotion by having a great story and great characters. Using cutesy techniques just for the sake of being different will get you rejected almost every time. Present tense is the most common of these "different for the sake of being different" techniques. While there are some novels that demand present tense to be told properly (*One Flew Over the Cuckoo's Nest*, for example), those novels are few. If you're telling your novel using present tense, make sure you have a reason that justifies the additional weight you've just added to your wagon. (Note that as more and more novels are written in present tense, this weight goes down. By the time you read this, this stone may be gone completely as it relates to present tense, but there are plenty more cutesy techniques waiting in the wings.)

Not enough dialogue in first few pages

To some extent, this stone is about present-day expectations. We live in a TV culture. Despite what many editors claim, if James Michener wrote a first novel today in the same style as *Hawaii* or *Centennial*, he'd probably earn a rejection slip. Modern readers are used to sound bites and videos. They don't want fifty pages of info dumps to start their novels. Even ignoring these expectations, there are good reasons to have dialogue in the first few pages of your novel. Readers want story and characters. That means they want conflicts and relationships. It's hard to reveal relationships without other characters present, and it's hard to have other characters present while trying to reveal those relationships, and yet have no dialogue. The random musings of a solitary character are never as interesting as that same character engaged in a dynamic conversation with another character, because that dynamic conversation reveals a relationship between the characters. If your opening scene is active or interesting enough, sometimes dialogue isn't needed, but not having any dialogue is still a stone in your wagon.

<u>Not enough action in first few pages</u>

This item is closely related to the last item. Story and characters means conflicts and relationships. You can describe conflicts without having any action, but it's almost always more interesting to reveal conflicts through character actions rather than laying those conflicts at the readers' feet like a package of rotting fish. Sure, the reader knows they're there, but they're not very appealing. Have your protagonist actively interacting with other characters on page one of your novel and your wagon will be that much lighter.

And all the rest

Enough stones exist that I could fill this book talking about them. I singled out the ones above because they're the most common, or because they appear so often in published fiction that many beginning writers mistakenly believe the rules are the same for them as they are for established authors.

In truth, every editor has a personalized set of stones they drop in your wagon as soon as they see they'll fit there.

For example, including a personalized cover letter with your manuscript causes some editors to drop a stone in your wagon. Failure to include such a cover letter causes other editors to put in a stone. Sometimes the stones stop your wagon in its tracks. REJECT appears on its sides and down the hill it comes. The editors never see your stellar prose in chapter two. They never reach the awesome idea you reveal halfway through your first chapter. Your brilliantly witty dialogue on page five is never read. The instant some editors see you start with a prologue or see you're using present tense, they reach for the form rejection letter. You're not getting published with them. If they decide your viewpoint character is unsympathetic, they stop reading. If they catch three grammar mistakes by the end of page two, they never reach page three. You get the idea, but I can't stress this enough. Most manuscripts are rejected in seconds. You can do everything else perfectly, but if your first page is awful, it's extremely unlikely any editor will ever read your manuscript because they've decided your fate before you get the chance to prove them wrong. Give yourself the best chance to get published by keeping that wagon empty.

Literary Agents

Most writers picture an agent (or editor) as a writer's friend, that person who meets you for lunch and gives you encouragement and advice. They take care of your cat when you have to suddenly fly off to Columbia and rescue your sister from a bunch of ruthless killers. The strange truth is that some writers do have agents who are indeed their friends. Some do provide help, constructive advice, and make a real difference in a writer's career. And then there's everybody else.

Like every other aspect of writing, how much an agent (or editor) is there for you nearly always depends on how much money you've made for that person. Those friends I mentioned above are typically agents (or editors) for bestselling writers. If you're a beginner, chances are you're not going to get much of anything. If you rely on them to take care of your cat, the poor feline is probably going to die. And the odds don't look good for your sister either.

So why get an agent? What use are they?

You certainly don't want them negotiating your contracts for you without looking over their shoulder. And they won't sell your novel for you. Only you (and your novel) can do that. Typically agents know the market better than you ever will (where the market in this case is the publishing houses, the editors who work for them, and possibly what projects they have in the works). Agents also tend to keep a pretty close eye on the money stream after publication. After all, they want paid, too.

That's the minor stuff. For a beginning writer, an agent really earns their money in only one way: They are the only person who can reliably get your novel in front of many different editors in an amazingly short amount of time.

So is this service worth fifteen percent? Absolutely— for your first novel. Without the agent, you probably don't get published—or you wait years to get published. But if your first novel was the first book in a twenty-book series, chances are good the agent just landed the big one. I'm not saying they don't do anything valuable for those other nineteen novels—they certainly will—but whether it's worth fifteen percent of every dollar you are paid is highly questionable. Agents know this, too, which is why most have contracts that make it difficult to dump them when the going gets good.

I'm not saying that agents don't earn their money. They do. For every novel they sell, they have to handle a ton of turkeys that don't make them a dime. They need to know their markets, maintain contacts in an ever- and rapidly-changing publishing world, and wear a lot of different hats based on what task they're tackling. Why shouldn't they get a big payday when one of those turkeys grows up to be a soaring Hollywood eagle or a perennial bestseller?

Despite all the good things an agent may do for a beginning writer, the only practical reason I can recommend for attempting to get one is the ability to speed up the decision process. In essence, you're hiring an agent for their ability to get that "no" that allows you to move on to the next market.

If you want to sell to the traditional houses, a good agent will give you a better chance to do so. So how do you get a good agent? Can you go online and order one from Agents-R-Us? Not quite. But it's getting closer to that all the time.

Finding an Agent

Like the publishing world, the world of literary agents is ever-changing. That means all of the information in this section is subject to change. Still, the methods outlined here will probably be the same for some time to come. Even so, mentally place "At the time of this writing…." in front of all of the suggestions given below. (It was good advice when I wrote it.)

The process of finding an agent is not a trivial one. You've spent hundreds—more likely thousands—of hours writing your novel. Do the work needed to create a list of competent agents who might be interested in your novel.

The best way to find an agent who might be right for you is the same place we tend to go for everything else: Online.

The best resource I found for researching agents online was QueryTracker (http://querytracker.net). The site is well organized, seems to have good information, and is relatively easy to use. The basic site is free and the premium site was only $25/year. From my perspective, this is the main site you should use to find agents to query.

One of the site's most useful features is under Agents in the top menu bar called "Who Reps Whom." Besides getting their grammar right, this function allows you to find out who represents your favorite authors. If you're on the path to success, you're writing novels that you would like to read yourself. Knowing which agents represent books you like to read gives you a huge advantage in finding an agent who might want to represent you and who has proven they can represent the kind of books you write.

Once you've identified every agent who looks like a good fit for you and your novel, another site can be useful for gathering information about that agent from an agent's or editor's point-of-view. The Publisher's Marketplace (http://www.publishersmarketplace.com) is designed specifically for publishing professionals (meaning agents, editors, and their support staff). Again, the best features of this site come with a paid membership, which is $25/ *month*. However, for an aspiring writer trying to find out about editors and agents, a one or two month membership should be sufficient to gather the information you need.

For both of the above sites, you can start out with the free version and make the decision to upgrade to the paid version on your own.

A free resource exists for finding out if an agent you've identified can be trusted. Writer Beware gives information on dangers that writers face, such as untrustworthy agents, scams, and fraud. There are many people and organizations that prey on new writers and on their desire to be published. The Writer Beware can help you avoid some of these pitfalls. These dangers go beyond agents and you should familiarize yourself with the dangers out there.

To avoid scams, follow this key guideline when examining any opportunity: Money flows toward the writer. That means people give you money, not the other way around. If you ever find yourself tempted to spend money because someone promises you they can get your novel published, you are almost certainly being taken advantage of. Run away! Run away fast!

Another couple sites have some useful information:

- AgentQuery.com (http://www.AgentQuery.com)
- Writers Market (http://www.WritersMarket.com)

Since the internet is an ever-changing landscape, your mileage may vary concerning these sites, but a couple

Google searches and a few hours you'll never get back should provide you with your own set of the latest and greatest resources for finding agents.

Eeny, Meeny, Miny, Moe, Catch an Agent by the Toe

Agents are shy creatures, seldom seen in daylight and extraordinarily difficult to catch in the wild. Rumor holds that they can be trapped by offering them free lunches and plying them with rounds of alcohol, but since most dwell only in the dark boroughs of New York City, not all of us have the budget to lead a safari into their natural habitat.

While it can indeed be beneficial to meet an agent face-to-face, the classic way to introduce yourself to an agent is through the venerable query letter. In today's world, those query letters are sometimes query emails, but don't underestimate the power of paper. Agents get hundreds of emails today. Why? Because email is easy: Once written, emails cost nothing to generate and send. But letters require work. They require postage. Like the use of typewriters in the age before computers, the effort and expense required to produce a physical query letter guarantees that any prospective agent will receive less physical query letters than they do electronic query letters.

The key to sending a physical query letter in today's world is to **not** include an SASE (self-addressed, stamped envelope), which is what we used to do in the old days. Instead, in your last paragraph, state specifically that you did not include an SASE. If they are interested in seeing a full or partial manuscript of your novel, please contact you at this email (or this phone number). If they are not interested in your novel, no response is required.

There may be a few crusty old agents who get offended by this no SASE inclusion, but for most agents, if they aren't interested in your novel, having your stated permission to toss your letter in the trash is a relief. It's what they were going to do anyway, so it's a nice feeling to have your permission. On the other hand, if they're interested in what you have, they'd rather email (or in rare instances, call) instead of producing a physical letter. We live in an electronic world. You can go outside of that in order to get noticed, but don't ask the agent to put in more work on your behalf. That way lies failure (and wasted stamps).

I'm Special and Here's Why

Have you ever watched a commercial on TV and found yourself wondering, "What the hell are they advertising?" This particular use of the Force must work on at least some of the weak-minded, or why would the marketers use it? For the rest of us, however, the ads that interest us most are ads that provide information about something we want. Maybe we want a cleaner house, a quieter car, cheaper insurance, or less-filling, tastes-great beer.

Most agents and editors would be more than happy to discover the next Dean Koontz, Stephen King or Nora Roberts. But when they read your query letter, they're a bit like a football fan on a Sunday afternoon: They've seen about all the beer commercials they can take. Your job as a writer is to convince them that you and your novel are worth their time.

But just like those ad agencies hawking beer, there are no guarantees. Almost every technique imaginable has worked at some point in time. And almost every technique imaginable has failed. Being especially cute or inventive could work for you, but it's extremely risky. And unlike those folks selling beer, you have an extremely limited set of buyers for your wares. You can literally query every potential market that exists for your novel. That's how few there are.

That means that unlike those commercials mentioned above, you want the person reading your letter to know exactly what you are advertising. The following guidelines provide a safe and reliable approach to querying agents and editors. That doesn't mean you can't be creative or that you should be boring. Be efficient. Be clear. Be interesting. Be informative.

Above all, remember that your query letter is nothing more than a commercial for you and your novel.

The Perfect Query Letter

Take the following information and make it your own. Remember, you're creating a written advertisement for you and your novel. This is equivalent to a TV ad marketing agency creating a TV ad for their services. What you're saying is important, but how you say it is important, too. What I give you below is the nuts and bolts. By necessity, the exact content of your query letter is left as an exercise for the reader—or in this case, the writer, meaning you.

Overall Advice

If you want an agent, your query letter will probably be the most important page you ever write. Be prepared to spend some time making it as good as it can be.

But what do I mean by good? Good is so subjective.

Let's look at it from the agent's point-of-view: You're a relatively successful agent with a few good clients, a few mediocre clients, and other clients who haven't made you any money yet. You get contacted by existing clients and editors, all of which expect a timely response. You need to keep up on all the latest publishing news because the one constant in the publishing industry is that it changes quickly. You also have your job as collection agent which includes reviewing royalty statements and pressuring publishers to find out why your authors haven't been paid on time and oh by the way when can you expect the check? You might submit a book proposal or two, follow up on submitted proposals, placate existing clients who need you for one thing or another, and work on ways to increase revenue for existing clients.

Notice that your focus is on the money because that's how you make your living. Granted, you need new clients from time to time because the existing ones die, quit writing, quit selling, or move on to other representation. But on a day-to-day basis you're not acquiring new clients. If you did, you'd be permanently overwhelmed by new clients within weeks.

So what do you want in a query letter from a prospective client? You want to know that there's a good chance any time you spend on them will pay off. And how can it possibly pay off? They give you a manuscript you can sell. More than that, this will be the first of many high-quality manuscripts they'll provide that will make you a good living for years to come. That means this writer seems professional, competent, and low-maintenance.

For you, as the writer, it means your query letter needs to be:

1) Interesting
2) Efficient
3) Clear
4) Enticing
5) Lucky

The benefits of the first four items should be self-explanatory. As for the last item, your letter needs to be lucky, because even if you write the perfect novel and have the perfect query letter to accompany it, there's an excellent chance the agent you're querying isn't accepting new clients.

What To Include

In your query, include the following:

- Who you are

- What you want (representation)
- Your novel's plot summed up in a single sentence
- Why makes your book a good read
- What qualifies you to write this book
- An offer to send your completed manuscript
- A thank you to the agent for considering your request

The first two items above encapsulate the most basic tenets of cold calling (which is very much the function a query letter performs). Agents need to know you're not trying to sell them Amway products or office supplies. Beyond that, if you can't articulate why they would want you as a client, you probably won't be one. They should understand immediately that you're seeking representation but they also need a reason to keep reading. That's why you tell them why your novel is a novel that will sell, not only to the publishing houses but to the readers, too.

The next to last item is vital. The agent must have no doubt that your novel is finished and ready to sell. The last item is just common courtesy.

In addition to the items above, if a reason exists for your selecting this particular agent, tell them what it is. "My novel is a paranormal western romance. Since you've represented <Author #1> and <Author #2> who also write in this genre, I selected you as the agent best suited to represent my work." Giving specific examples like the one above make your letter personal in a way that will easily allow it to stand out from the crowd. Also, it shows you've done your homework, meaning you know what you're doing in your quest to find an agent. If you know what you're doing in the sales part of the business, it bodes well for you knowing what you're doing in the writing end of the business. Plus everyone likes to feel appreciated. By knowing about the agent's previous work, it shows you've taken an interest in them, which makes them inclined to take an interest in you. But be careful with this one. It's nearly impossible to BS your way into saying why you chose a particular agent if you just grabbed their name because it was the next one on the list.

Know Who You're Writing

Don't step on the agent's face. If you're asking someone to enter into a business relationship—especially one as risky as publishing—the least you can do is get to know the basics about the person on the other end of the request. That means addressing them by name, spelling their name right, and getting their gender right. Doing these represent a minimal level of common courtesy that you should always do whether you're writing an agent or writing anybody else. With the wealth of information available on the internet, you should be able to accomplish all of these easily enough. On the off chance you simply cannot get confirmation of the agent's gender, address the agent by their full name, such as "Dear Jessie R. Agent."

Pointers

Most of the items below are issues of quality. You want your letter to be as engaging as possible without forgetting that it's a business letter with a specific purpose. This is where it would help to be an accomplished ad executive.

- Keep your query brief and to the point (no more than 500 words). If you're sending a physical letter rather than an email, your query should fit on a single page. If you're sending an email, it's best to make it even shorter. Busy people have less patience with electronic communication than they do written letters.

- Construct a friendly and lively letter that captures a bit of your style as well as the essence of your novel. Include humor if possible but avoid being cute.
- Give the agent a reason to request your full manuscript by creating an intriguing impression of your high quality, interesting, marketable novel.
- Remember that you're writing a business letter. If it's a physical letter, get your formatting right. If it's an email, keep your subject short and treat it like the title it is (meaning follow rules for capitalization). Make the subject line specific. You want it to be caught by filters if the agent has set them up. For example: "Established Author Seeking Representation for Paranormal Western Romance" Also, avoid attachments. Most agents have been burned too many times by virus-laden attachments to open yours.
- Don't provide too much information. Often less is more. You want the agent interested, which means rousing their curiosity, not satisfying it.
- Exactly follow any submission guidelines an agency provides. If they've taken the time to create the guidelines, they expect and require them to be followed. Sort of following them (or following most of them) doesn't count.

If you want an agent, your query letter will probably be the most important page you ever write. Be prepared to spend some time making it as good as it can be.

First Sentence

Start your letter with a powerful first sentence. Give your future agent a reason to keep reading. Most of the time that means you're providing a one-sentence summary of your novel or revelation of your unique abilities as a writer.

For example, the easiest way to get an agent is to sell a novel before you write your query letter. The greatest opening line to a query is: "I've just received a six-figure offer for my latest novel *I'm Going To Be Rich* from Moneybags Press, Inc. and I'm seeking representation." You could add another sentence about how you've reviewed the work of several agents and you've selected this lucky recipient to negotiate your deal, but honestly, that's not necessary. You had the agent hooked at "six-figure offer." A writer can have no better qualities in an agent's mind that an already sold novel seeking someone to receive the accompanying and hefty commission check. Granted, if you've received a three-figure offer, don't bother writing. For four- and five-figure offers, you should provide a few additional sentences of your exact circumstances, but let's face it: If you've already sold your novel, you have no problems—or at least no problems that any beginning writer wouldn't be happy to trade you for.

The second easiest way to keep an agent reading your query letter is to mention meeting them last week and how much you enjoyed that delicious dinner you shared (meaning: you paid for). Of course, this only works if you actually met them and took them to dinner. But this is also the place where you'd mention if anyone had recommended you contact them. For example, one of the surest ways to garner serious consideration for your query letter is to have one of the agent's top existing clients put in a good word on your behalf. Most agents don't have a ton of faith in their writers being able to spot other good writers, but it's a recommendation nonetheless. Also, it comes from a client they care about. If asked, they want to be able to respond intelligently about why they asked to see your sample chapters or why they (regretfully) had to turn you away. That's a huge advantage when it comes to getting your entire query letter read and considered.

In the extremely likely scenario you have no famous writer contacts to recommend you and you haven't already sold your novel (and therefore have an immediate desire to pay out a guaranteed commission fee), start with whatever is most likely to hook your agent's interest.

If you're a published writer, start with that. For example, if you've sold eight stories to several major market magazines or anthologies, agents will respect that. It means someone out there has already selected and paid for your work as a writer. On the other hand, if you're a self-published writer, don't mention that unless you've been wildly successful. The latter is unlikely if you're seeking an agent. The exception falls under the first scenario above. Also don't brag about any publications by non-paying or low-paying markets. Like anyone who works for a living, agents want to make money. Knowing you sold a piece for $10 to a church weekly run by your Aunt Flo isn't going to impress anyone. Mention any publications if you have any, but only lead with experience that will help you sell your novel.

For example, if you're writing a political suspense novel and you served as President Obama's Executive Clerk for three years, you have immediate credibility as a writer who knows inside information other writers don't. The same goes if you're a retired police officer writing a police procedural or a NASA engineer writing a novel about space colonization. Granted, being too much of an expert can backfire. Most people who live the life can't write about the life but often try. Still, if the one-sentence summary of your novel reveals your understanding of drama and character, having real-life credentials can set you apart from an equally good query writer who doesn't have those credentials.

Now, for everyone else. You know, the writers who aren't already wildly successful or uniquely qualified. In other words, normal beginning writers, or as I like to call them, future best-selling authors. If you fall into this category, you need to sell novels based on how interesting (and marketable) you can make your novel sound. That means you better have written a great novel and you better be able to capture the essence of that greatness in a couple sentences. If that's the case, don't draw attention to your lack of expertise or experience. Let your novel do the talking (and selling).

If you fall into this most common category, start your query letter with a one-sentence summary. This summary sentence should stand on its own and generate an impression of your book that gives people a reason to buy and read your novel.

One-Sentence Summary

All published writers should have a one-sentence summary handy for each of their books. It's an important and powerful marketing technique that's covered in detail as part of our section on "Marketing." For now, I'll give you the basics that apply specifically to query letters. Your one-sentence summary should provide the following information:

- Your novel's genre
- Your main character
- Your overall story
- The struggle

This information isn't told directly. You reveal this information through your summary sentence. For example, whatever character you mention is your main character. The genre is revealed by the story and the struggle.

Notice that I've said nothing about needing to reveal your theme. "My novel's about a boy's struggle to discover his inner adult." Okay, maybe that would catch someone's attention. Most themes are more typical and therefore won't help sell anything: Coming of age, love triumphs all, evil doesn't pay, only good vampires sparkle—whatever.

I also didn't mention anything about accuracy. While your one-sentence summary should capture the spirit of your story and the struggle, of necessity it will be incomplete. That means that if your second, more minor storyline is much more interesting than your main storyline, you talk about it instead. After all, story's in the eye of the beholder. Take *Gone with the Wind* as an example:

- A southern woman struggles to find love during and after the devastation of the Civil War
- An entrepreneurial renegade battles against the traditional, male-dominated businesses who control the economic climate in Atlanta after the Civil War
- Following the North's successful war of independence for southern slaves, a manipulative southern belle teases and traps multiple husbands on her way to economic security and eventual tragedy

- A resourceful and desperate mother's bid to retain her childhood home reveals the glory of the Old South as told by people who were there

All of these summaries are accurate at some level. Decide on your novel's best target audience and tailor your first sentence toward them.

The best way to get a grip on one-sentence summaries is by reading (and writing) one-sentence summaries. Here are a few examples:

- Trapped on an island, eight strangers are murdered one by one as the survivors struggle to discover whom among them is the killer. (Agatha Christie's *And Then There Were None*)
- A young Hobbit battles evil foes on his treacherous journey to rid the world of a ring so powerful it could destroy all good in Middle Earth. (J. R. R. Tolkien's *The Lord of the Rings*)
- A young orphan boy discovers he's a wizard and must use his new-found powers to stop the evil tyrant who murdered his parents. (J. K. Rowling's *Harry Potter and the Philosopher's Stone*)
- A Harvard symbologist battles an ancient and deadly religious sect to decode complicated clues that lead to the powerful truth about Jesus Christ. (Dan Brown's *The Da Vinci Code*)
- A regretful pedophile struggles to control and isolate his twelve-year-old stepdaughter who both loathes him and relishes the power her sexual favors cast over him. (Vladimir Nabokov's *Lolita*)

First of all, if you want to be a best-selling novelist but haven't read any of these novels (or series of novels), you should get busy and do so. Depending on what source you reference, these novels have sold between 50 million and 150 million copies each. As an aspiring writer, you should understand why they were so successful.

As you examine the above examples, you should be able to identify the novel's genre, main character(s), and overall story and struggle for each. In no cases is anything told directly, not even genre. If the agent can't tell what the genre is from your one-sentence summary, you probably haven't written it correctly.

After a similar fashion, only specify setting if it matters. It could be argued that it isn't necessary for Agatha Christie's *And Then There Were None*, but in my opinion, specifying the strangers were trapped on an island heightens the suspense and answers many questions. Well worth the four words that information costs.

Notice that all the examples above are less than 30 words long. The majority are less than 25. A good target length is 25 words or less. For most novels, you can't capture an interesting impression in less than 15 words, but if you can make it happen, go for it.

> A spelling spider saves a friendly pig from slaughter (E. B. White's Charlotte's Web)

For myself, this nine-word summary gives an impression of the novel, but it doesn't capture the wonder or generate interest as well as a somewhat more wordy summary could.

Remember, you're not trying to tell what your book's about in the shortest way possible; you're trying to sell your novel using the fewest words needed. There's a difference.

For your own summary, weigh every word. Your sentence should read well. If it takes 32 words to make that happen, don't sweat the extra words. No one else will.

For a Few Sentences More

Feel free to expand on your opening sentence. If you wrote about yourself and your unique ability to capture the novel, feel free to add more credentials. If you provided a one-sentence summary of your novel, add a few more sentences to increase interest. The main caution I give is to use these sentences well. They're not filler. They're a few sentences more that you allow yourself as a way to sell what you've written. Take *The Lord of the Rings* example from above.

> A young Hobbit battles evil foes on his treacherous journey to rid the world of a ring so powerful it could destroy all good in Middle Earth.

What's a Hobbit? What's Middle Earth? Rings don't have power in the real world, so this novel is clearly fantasy. But what kind? High fantasy? Epic fantasy? One possible way to complete your opening paragraph would be with the following sentences:

> A tale of traditional fantasy based on Nordic mythology, the rich world of Middle Earth boasts Hobbits, elves, dwarves, trolls, orcs, goblins, and men as well as scores of magical creatures such as dragons, monstrous spiders, giant eagles, and more. Driven by the timeless struggle of good vs. evil, giant armies clash while a lone Hobbit risks his soul and everything he loves in a desperate bid to restore order

> to a world dangling precariously on the
> brink of destruction.

These additional sentences give the agent valuable information. They paint a portrait of a detailed world with plenty of potential as the setting for a lengthy (and profitable) series. They solidify this novel's genre as epic fantasy and provide a reasonable impression of character conflict. What they don't do is provide much information about the story beyond the most basic of basics. Remember, your query letter is a marketing tool. You're not trying to tell the agent what your novel's about; you're trying to sell your novel. Intrigue them. Spark enough interest that they request sample chapters and/or an outline.

The same holds true if your opening sentence focused on you. Only expand it if you have more credentials that increase the agent's interest. If not, it's time to move on to the novel.

Body of the Letter

How you started the letter will determine how you continue the letter. If your first paragraph focused on something other than your novel, your second will focus on your novel's plot, characters, and story. If you focused on the novel to start the letter, focus now on yourself and why you'll be a client they want to have.

When the agent finishes reading your letter, it's true that they should believe they know what your book is about. The beauty of a query letter is that you tweak and adjust and rewrite your letter until it hums. It needs to flow as naturally as possible, but it should pack a powerful informational and emotional punch. You want the agent (and eventually the editors and the readers) to think that this sounds like a great novel.

Granted, the main criteria that determines whether someone wants to read a particular book is often personal taste. You can't worry about that. The book is already written. Your job is to make it sound as interesting as possible without worrying about whether a single reader likes that type of novel. As far as your agent goes, if you did your research before starting your search, you should have identified agents that represent the type of novel you've written. Given that, your job is then to show that this particular novel is marketable. The only reliable way to do that is to tell them what your novel's about in an interesting way.

Get In and Get Out

Your letter now has information about your book and about yourself. In most cases, that's all you have to offer. Offer to send them your completed manuscript and thank them for their consideration. Every agent I've ever encountered valued brevity in a query letter. This is not the time to be chatty. They may well give you a call to ask questions about your novel and evaluate your engaging personality, but don't try to capture that in a query letter.

Remember, agents almost never agree to represent a writer from a query letter alone. (The exception would most often be the query letter that starts with, "I've just received a six-figure offer for my latest novel....") The query letter should tell them just enough to pique their interest and no more. After all, the more you say, the more chance you have to reveal something that would make them decide they don't want to represent you.

Get It Down

Often the best way to write a query letter is to write an initial version that is longer than the final version. Concentrate on making it interesting. Include everything you'd like to tell the agent. Tell them all about your novel. Brag up how you discovered yourself as a writer when you were trapped in the ceiling above your grade school during a fire drill. Then trim, trim, compress, sharpen, and trim. Make it short without losing anything important.

An Agent, an Editor, a Candlestick Maker

Note that all of the advice I've given for writing a query letter to an agent applies to writing a query letter to a book editor with the exception that you're asking for publication consideration instead of representation. The same basic principles would apply if you wanted to submit a short story to a closed market. In all cases you're writing a commercial for yourself.

My First Agent

I was fortunate enough early in my career to snag a professional New York agent with the query letter that appears on the next page. This is a good demonstration of the edict: "Do as I say, not as I do." I don't include this query letter as a good example (although it may give you hope that any query letter you write can't be any worse). In particular, the body of query letter is much too long and complicated. To no one's surprise but mine, the novel mentioned herein never sold.

So why was the agent interested? Getting a straight answer out of most agents about such a subject is well nigh impossible, but my own guess is that my credentials were the selling point. I was a published short story author, which proved to the agent that I could write at some minimum level of competence. I was a full member of the Science Fiction Writers of America (now Science Fiction & Fantasy Writers of America), which meant I'd had at least three professional sales. One of my published stories had been singled out for favorable review by a professional reviewer. It was enough that this agent wanted to see some sample chapters and a synopsis.

A synopsis! How do you write that? We'll cover that in the next section.

G. R. Sixbury
2100 Lonely Lane
Emerald City, OZ 66699
<<Today's Date>>

<<Agent Name>>
<<Agent Address>>
<<Agent City, State, Zip>>

Dear <<Agent First Name>>:

I am seeking representation for my fantasy novel, *Misthaven*. I am a published author and belong to SFWA.

My novel is set on Misthaven (a world of my creation). The story revolves around four powerful characters: Mykon, Jep, Vel, and Bramon (an off-worlder). Mykon and Jep are half-brothers, grandsons and heirs to King Gabel of Westplains. When Mykon kills his grandfather using an ancient potion, he accidentally creates a plague that ravages the planet. Fearing their people will perish, leaders from the six lands of Misthaven band together. Jep convinces them their only solution is to capture Mykon and force him to give them the cure. They do not know that Mykon has not yet found an antidote to the disease or that Jep is interested more in revenge. Vel, matriarchal leader of the Delrabo, married Mykon the winter after he killed King Gabel and warns him of Jep's plan. Bramon, a graduate student from University Station, is sent to the primitive world of Misthaven to join a small anthropological study team, but his shuttle crashes and he is captured by the group of leaders traveling north to find Mykon. Vel falls in love with

Bramon and is torn by her secret marriage to Mykon and Bramon's desire to stay with the lead group as they travel North to Mykon's stronghold.

Misthaven is not a novel of elves, gnomes, or dragons. Rather, its fantasy element is provided by Giftusers. These special individuals have trained for years to enhance their natural mental abilities. Using these gifts, they can lift objects, change an object's shape, see objects at a molecular level, teleport themselves over small distances, or read someone's mind. Each Giftuser has only one of the above abilities. Traditionally, they are the leaders of their homelands. Jep and Vel are Giftusers. Mykon is an *Ekarlan* (a scientist). For generations, many Giftusers have feared the *Ekarlans*, realizing the devices these scientists create could become as powerful as their mental gifts. Because Bramon is captured near his wrecked shuttle, he is also labeled an *Ekarlan*.

My best-known story, "Circles", was published in *Four Moons of Darkover* in November, 1988. I have enclosed a review of this anthology.

Upon request, I will send you all or any part of the manuscript for *Misthaven*. Thank you for your time and your consideration.

Sincerely,

G. R. Sixbury

A Sellable Synopsis

So an agent's interested. That's great. But instead of (or in addition to) your entire manuscript, they want to see a synopsis of your novel. Now what?

For your sake, you should have written the synopsis before sending off your first query letter. While it's theoretically possible to write a great synopsis in a single evening, synopses are a lot like query letters. Each word should be crafted for maximum effect. Whereas your query letter was a 30-second ad for your novel, your synopsis is more of an infomercial. Your audience is interested. They want to know more, a lot more. Now's your chance to show off all the cool bells and whistles of this new-fangled novel thing you've created. But make no mistake. It's still an advertisement for your novel.

Just to make it a bit more confusing, the agent (or editor) might ask for an outline of your novel. Nearly all of the time, when they say outline, they mean synopsis. So what's a synopsis?

What It Is; What It Ain't

I feel like I'm repeating myself, because I am, but it can't be stressed enough. When it comes to writing a synopsis, most authors go astray because they don't understand what a synopsis is. It's a commercial for your book. Nothing more. Nothing less. The synopsis must sell the novel, it doesn't need to be accurate. Sure, you're trying to give a relatively truthful impression of your book. If you've written a novel about monkey-eating space aliens, don't write a synopsis about giant desert-dwelling worm babies whose byproducts power the universe. But don't let your synopsis be tied down by your novel, either. A synopsis must stand on its own as a unique and compelling version of the story you're telling. It should seem larger than life, and everything in it more important than it actually is. The synopsis is a mere shadow of the book, so exaggerate the synopsis to give it depth.

Go all out to sell your story. Distort the synopsis as much as needed to make it read smoothly and read fast. All (and I stress the word *all*) that you're trying to do with a synopsis is convince the reader that your book is great and wonderful. Best book ever!

Overview

In simplest terms, a synopsis is a two to twenty page summary of your book that covers the basic plot, possibly the theme, and typically reveals the ending. The synopsis should flow well, must be interesting, and should be a quick, easy read. A synopsis is as brief as possible to convey the information needed, but should not be choppy or confusing. It should reveal the main thrust of your story, the setting, the motivation of the characters, the scope of the novel, and provide some idea of the novel's overall structure.

Feel Your Way

A synopsis should flow as smoothly as possible. Don't reveal any jagged edges that could catch a reader's attention and stop them in their tracks. In a perfect synopsis, there is no chance for the reader to quit reading. It flows so well and reads so quickly the reader is done before they realize it. As such, get rid of any details that cloud the plot. Also, feel free to bend the plot into whatever shape makes it the most interesting. The people who are reading your synopsis aren't going to go back and compare your synopsis to the finished manuscript and scold you for any differences. They're reading the synopsis simply as a time saver. If it took the same amount of time to read your novel as it took to read your synopsis, they'd read your novel instead. It's the novel they're buying, not the synopsis.

Length

Writers spout a variety of truths regarding synopses. In all honesty, a good synopsis is one that sells. Nothing more than that. As such, it needs to be as long as it takes in order to sell the associated novel it represents. I've had editors and agents tell me they never want to read a synopsis more than five pages long. I've had others insist that a good synopsis is often 20 pages long. The real answer is that **everyone prefers something different.** There is no firm guideline. In my own research related to synopses, most professional authors I've talked with tend to hover around the 6 - 10 page mark (single-spaced). If you're looking for a hard and fast rule about length, you won't find an accurate one. If you want a general guideline, I'd recommend 5 - 15 pages (single spaced). Note that many long-published authors will provide much shorter synopses and might recommend you do the same. The problem is that editors and agents trust experienced, selling authors more than they do beginning writers. A Stephen King written synopsis will sell because it's Stephen King. You don't have that luxury.

Tense

Often synopses are done in present tense. Think about someone you know who is an entertaining verbal storyteller. Often they use present tense. "I'm going to the zoo and I see this giraffe. He's standing right in the middle of the freeway, his tongue reaching up and licking one of those new, green cars that's trapped on the overpass, stuck in traffic. The giraffe thinks it's some kind of leafy tree, see?" Present tense is a faster, more immediate telling of a story than past tense. While most people don't prefer present tense for a novel length manuscript, it tends to work well for synopses. However, if your synopsis reads better to you in past tense, do it that way. There are no hard and fast rules.

Spacing

My page lengths in the "Length" section are based on single-spaced pages, but it doesn't mean synopses must be single-spaced. Manuscripts are double-spaced so that an editor or a copy editor can mark up a printed version of the manuscript. Synopses are not for publication. As such, they aren't edited. This gives an author the freedom to single-space the synopsis, which produces a more a finished book appearance. In the old days, it also saved on postage.

Dare Not the Chapter Follow

Under no normal circumstance should a synopsis slavishly follow a chapter-by-chapter approach. Using a chapter-by-chapter synopsis is probably the best way to write a synopsis that will *never* sell your novel. If you find a source that recommends a chapter by chapter synopsis, I would ignore everything that source says about synopses. The only time to use a chapter-by-chapter synopsis is when you are specifically asked to do so by an agent. Sometimes agents say outline when they mean synopsis, so clarifying is both prudent and advisable. If the agent really is requesting a true chapter by chapter outline, I would question the validity of the agent.

Synopses are Recyclable

The same synopsis is generally appropriate for both agents and editors. You are trying to sell the novel to both of them. You aren't trying to tell either of them what the book is actually about or how it's actually put together. Barring some inside information about the preferences of a particular agent or a particular editor, the sales synopsis will be the same for both.

It Bears Repeating

The sole purpose of your synopsis is to sell your novel. It is a marketing tool. Car dealers sell cars. Clerks in a clothing stores sell clothes. Writers sell books. The difference is that most car dealers don't manufacture the cars they sell, but they did in the earliest days of car manufacturing. In a perfect world, writers could simply write books. When we finished, we could post an ad on Craigslist or eBay and when an editor or an agent wanted a book, they would look us up and order one. It doesn't work that way. Instead, writers have to wear multiple hats. First, we must write the novels we want to sell. Then we must sell them. When we go the traditional publishing route, we have to sell the same novel multiple times to different types of audiences: First to an agent, second to an editor, and third to the general public. At least writers are selling a product they can believe in, because if you don't believe in your own product, you need to start by first creating a product you do believe in. And if you do believe in the product, why wouldn't you want to sell it? That's the best part about a writer's sales job: You're supplying something agents, editors, and readers need and want, which means you're helping them.

Synopses are Tools

Few hard and fast rules exist regarding synopses. They were invented as a time-saver. Agents and editors sometimes need new clients and new novels to sell, but they don't have time to read every book they need to consider in order to find the ones they need. Synopses provide a shortcut to reading the whole work. In rare circumstances, agents and editors sometimes get all the information they need in order to make an acceptance decision based on the synopsis alone. Usually, the purpose of the synopsis is to justify the time needed to read the entire book.

Nuts and Bolts

A synopsis is nearly always pure narration (with the exception of a line or two of dialogue or a very short partial scene). This means you're allowed to state things directly if it makes sense to do so. "Sandy is the heroine. Teri is the villain." Your main emphasis should focus on relational conflicts, not problems. You're pitting character against character.

Beginning

Most synopses start in one of three ways: 1) An overall one-paragraph summary of the novel followed by the full synopsis summary, 2) The extended novel summary starting at the beginning and going to the end, and 3) A "jacket blurb" paragraph, then the novel summary. With all three techniques, you should take care to summarize the material contained in the sample chapters, so that any synopsis reader can tell how the sample chapters fit within the novel. At the same time, avoid including a disproportionate share of your first chapter in the synopsis (what many editors call

"First Chapter Syndrome"). Jump right into the story and keep the story moving all the way to the end.

Middle

Condense chapters down to a paragraph, a few sentences, or even half a line. Stress what's most dramatic about your novel and let explanations slide as much as possible. Most editors/agents don't care about the reasons why something works. An old joke starts with, "What does the rocket ship in your novel run on?" Answer: "Fuel." Said another way, reduce complexity as much as possible. Keep the basic idea and trim the rest. If you say your group of adventurers jumps into a worm hole and re-emerges on the other side of the galaxy, agents/editors assume you will make this convincing in your novel. You can't make it convincing in your synopsis, so don't try. If some technical or explanatory detail can't be avoided, sum it up in a sentence, if possible. If necessary, include a whole paragraph. If you find yourself needing more background than that, rewrite the story contained in the synopsis so that you don't need that much explanation.

Your characters' motivations and actions should be clear in a synopsis. Even if you think it's a good idea to confuse your reader in the novel regarding whether they should root for or against a character, don't do it the synopsis. You also don't want any confusion about the characters' actions. It should be clear what the characters did, when they did it, and why. This goes for villains as well as heroes.

Since lengthy explanations and subtlety don't work well in a synopsis, be wary of situations that make it sound as if your character is saved when the cavalry comes charging over the hill or is saved in some sudden and unexpected way, even if this is what really happens. While the long version of these events often work, they too often sound like *deus ex machina* in a synopsis.

If you have any unexplained or seemingly irrelevant events happen in your sample chapters, make sure that these are covered by your synopsis. For example, if you have a main character leave in chapter two, have a line in your synopsis like, "Main Heroine Two goes back to Tennessee to live with her ailing mother but she will return in Chapter Fourteen." In essence, you're assuring them you know what you're doing; you've heard of Chekhov's Gun, which just means that if you have a loaded gun in the first act of your story, that gun will get fired (or play some other major part in your story) before you reach the end.

Ending

I've talked to dozens of editors who have emphasized that you ***must*** reveal your novel's ending in the synopsis. I've talked to a few others who've asked, "Who wants to know the ending of a mystery novel before they've read it?" Which advice you follow is your choice. One point in favor of not revealing your ending, especially for a good whodunit novel, is that your goal is to have the editor/agent read your entire manuscript. If the editor/agent loves everything else about your novel but you don't reveal the ending, I think most editors/agents will still request the manuscript. But what if they like everything else but don't *love* it? This is one of those areas where there is no correct answer. Use your best judgment.

Example Structure

One possible way to structure your synopsis starts with the single paragraph summary technique where you capture the entire novel. Follow that with an extended summary that comprises the rest of the novel. One way to summarize the novel is to show:

1) **Story:** The circumstances of characters and how those circumstances and character motivations create a great story.

2) **Relationships and Conflict:** Establish relationships of characters and show how those relationships create conflict.

3) **Change:** Show how events change relationships and what changes have occurred in the characters circumstances and relationships.

Throughout the rest of the synopsis, use transitions that introduce each of the next series of events by telling what those events do for the story.

Characters

Keep the number of characters mentioned by name (and places mentioned by name) as small as possible without causing confusion or requiring explanation. Introduce them with a line or two at most. When possible, let the characters' plot actions reveal their motivations.

The first time each character's name appears, capitalize it and identify your main viewpoint character(s) by placing (POV) behind their name. Weave the introduction of characters into the narration. Do not have a separate character sheet (or in general separate explanation sheets of any kind). Many editors hate this. Having said this, if you need either to tell your story, use them.

In general, it's impossible to capture intriguing characters in your synopsis. Instead of trying to recreate those characters in your synopsis, you use the characters to tell your story in the most interesting and dramatic way possible.

Big Action/Dramatic Scenes

The big moments—those parts of your novel that provide the reason most readers read and that keep them coming back for more—are nearly impossible to capture in a synopsis. Don't try. More than one editor has told me that for a big battle scene, they would prefer a single sentence such as "And then the climactic battle takes place." The same goes for a pivotal sex scene or a giant revelation. If you make it clear to the editor that you know what you're doing by stating with confidence what you're going to do, most editors take that as a sign of maturity and control and give you credit to pull off whatever scene you've just promised.

Extras

I always like to mix a bit of description and a snippet or two of dialogue into the synopsis narration just to break up the never-ending narration. You should try to give your synopsis some style without distracting from your story. In general, editors don't buy concepts; they buy story lines. Make sure you have a good story, and then make it sound as interesting and entertaining (and therefore marketable) as you can.

Book Proposal vs. Synopsis

Sometimes agents or editors ask for a book proposal instead of a synopsis and sample chapters. Normally one is just a shortcut for the other. Often a book proposal will include some kind of information about the writer, similar to what you might have put in your query letter. Obviously a novel proposal from an accomplished short story writer who's won multiple awards will carry more weight than a proposal from a complete unknown. Some beginning writers complain about this kind of favoritism, but it's just good business sense. Not only is it safer (at least one other professional has deemed this writer's work worthy of pay), but the awards indicate that some group somewhere thought the writer's work was worthy of recognition. Don't sweat it if they ask for a proposal. Just give them your synopsis, your sample chapters, and provide a cover letter that tells a little bit about yourself (and brags the novel up in some way).

<u>Sample Chapters</u>

While not part of the synopsis, sample chapters are usually paired with your synopsis to create the bulk of any book proposal. For sample chapters, always send the beginning of the novel (traditionally the first three chapters). Your target for length should be 10,000 – 15,000 words. Obviously you want to cut off the sample chapters at a point of high drama. Just as with any reader, you want to give your synopsis reader a desire to keep reading.

That's All There Is

A synopsis is much like a short story, similar in form (not in content or style!) to what a grandmother might tell her grandchildren at bedtime. Translated it comes out as: this is the situation, this is the hero, this is the villain, and this is what they do.

Remember, you are telling a story to an agent or editor with the intention that they will like your story so much, they will want to read it in its "unabridged" form.

Feel free to break any of the "rules" I've given above, provided you keep the synopsis clear, concise, and interesting. The only result you're seeking is for the agent/editor to want to read your novel. If that happens, the synopsis is a success.

After Your Novel Sells

You found an agent (or you didn't), your novel was sent to an editor at a major publishing company, and now the editor's contacted you with an offer. What now?

This is the situation you've been working toward since you first thought about writing a novel (whether you know it or not). But it's not the end. Instead it's the part that most authors don't care for: the business end of writing. Never fear. This minefield isn't nearly as hard to navigate as it might seem. But make no mistake: It is a minefield. Let me mark out a path for you so you don't blow your chance at fame and fortune with your first step.

The Contract

In a perfect world, once you received an offer to buy your book, your work would be done. This isn't true. Your first task is to make sure you don't give up the farm in exchange for seeing your novel on a bookstore shelf.

First, understand that most agents are lousy contract negotiators (for first novels). Typically the money isn't good, you don't have a track record, and all they see is 15% commission as a return on their investment of time and faith in an unproven writer.

Read your contract carefully. My first contract said specifically that I would write the novel, submit the novel, and if they didn't like it, they didn't have to pay. That seems reasonable. But it also said that regardless whether they paid me, they had full rights to use any and all of my work. What!? This means that, as written, I could write the novel and they could use it without paying me a dime. What's important here is that this contract was reviewed and okayed by my agent before I ever saw it. How did she miss this? Your guess is as good as mine, but I will always believe that she had other things on her mind and just didn't bother to read the contract all that carefully. No skin off her nose. (Actually, it would have been. If I didn't get paid, she wouldn't have been paid, either.)

And contracts aren't easy to read. They are conflicted (on purpose perhaps?). Typically provisions aren't organized in any reasonable way and sometimes clauses are contradictory. Read your contract carefully and make sure you understand every part of it. If you have any doubt, take the contract to a literary lawyer (a lawyer who specializes in matters related to the publishing industry). Most agents advise their clients in good faith, but the typical agent is not skilled at negotiating legal documents and doesn't understand the complex and legally binding clauses any better than you do.

So what are you looking for when you read the contract?

First, what rights are they buying?

If they're buying all rights, don't accept the contract as is. Make a counter offer to sell First American Serial Rights only. In particular, you don't want to give up on any income related to audible books, Braille, international, and above all, film options. Understand that if a publisher buys all rights, they buy all rights. You don't want to end up like Harland David Sanders (better known as Colonel Sanders), who was so excited about selling his restaurant franchise that he sold too many rights. Late in life, after earning only a fraction of the profits as Heublein, Inc. (the company he sold his company to), he wanted to start over. Only then did he discover that not only had he sold his chicken recipe, he had also sold his name. He was forced to open a restaurant under his wife's name (Claudia Sanders). Even with that change, Heublein sued the old Colonel and he was forced to sell the new restaurant.

If your publisher balks and insists on buying all rights, at the very least get an expiration date. Typically you can negotiate for a return of rights if the novel ever goes out of print or if sales dip below a certain number. Often your agent can be of use on such matters. Agents know that selling rights later means another paycheck for them.

The exception to negotiating regarding all rights is when you do a media tie-in novel or something similar. If you're writing in someone else's world, they will (and should) retain all rights to anything you produce. They invented the darned thing after all. In that case, you're doing what's known as work-for-hire. This is no different than a plumber being paid to come and fix your sink. You have work to do, you do it, you're paid for that work, and that's all you're entitled to. For a media tie-in novel, this all rights agreement makes sense. For nearly everything else, it's a fool's proposition.

After the Contract

Once the contract is signed, you are legally bound to abide by whatever it says. That means that if you weren't finished with the novel when it sold, the publishing house requested specific changes as a condition of purchase, or you've agreed to a seven-book series, you're obligated to deliver.

For example, I sold my first novel the year after losing both my mother and father within an 8-month span. Still reeling from my sudden status as an adult orphan and loaded down with family and work commitments, I somehow managed to sell this particular novel based on a synopsis alone. The publishing company gave me a generous six months to write, edit, and polish my novel. I had already agreed to be the head coach for my son's little league team and could not back out of it. Like all writers, these time stealers (called real life and being human) made the six-months goal an optimistic one. I agreed to this deadline in part because I didn't have much choice if I wanted to be published and because the publisher had sent me an example of the type of novel they were looking for that was only 70,000 words long. Surely I could finish a 70,000 word novel in six months. Unfortunately my contract specified that I would write a 100,000 word novel. I believed the example rather than the contract. My mistake.

As soon as I discovered my 30,000 word error in judgment, I adjusted my schedule accordingly. As you can imagine, finishing 100,000 words in six months given my other responsibilities was no easy task. Also, my writing future depended upon the quality of what I produced. On the other hand, several of my author friends would laugh at such a ridiculously long deadline for a single novel only 100,000 words long. It's all perspective.

When I was a couple months from the deadline, I realized having another 60 days to work on the novel would go a long way toward making it a much better novel. I forwarded this fact to my editor in an appeal for just a bit more time. He responded that I had signed a contract that called for a 100,000 word novel that would be finished on time and that they would love. Anything else would be a violation of my contract, which would then make it null and void.

Okay then.

I finished the novel on time. Then the editor sat on it for eight months before he bothered to read it.

Don't get me wrong. This was his right. The contract spelled out my responsibilities. I give this example to make it clear that common sense and logic are not necessarily related to a publishing contract. If you agreed to an obligation in your contract, you will be expected to fulfill that obligation regardless of health concerns, family emergencies, or sudden death. Granted, if you're dead, there's not a lot they can do to you. But based on my experience with large traditional publishing houses, you'll still be expected to fulfill your contract.

In addition to specific contract obligations, you may be expected to provide input for a back cover blurb, tag lines, a marketing synopsis, etc. You will sometimes be asked to fill out a new author questionnaire or solicit recommendations for your novel from other authors (hopefully best-selling authors that just happen to be your best buds). You may be asked for a head shot for publicity photos and you might be expected to set up signings, schedule interviews, craft news releases, and in all other ways do as much marketing as you can.

These obligations aren't always spelled out in your contract, but in general, they're in your best interest. They're aimed at selling your novel, and for many reasons, you want to sell your novel. One reason is that your performance on your first novel greatly affects whether you'll ever sell anything under your own name again. Many of the pseudonyms in the publishing industry came about because an author's last novel didn't earn enough money and publishing houses refused to consider any other work from that author. If you don't sell well under your own name, guess whose name you won't be selling under anymore?

There are also some practical obligations you must fulfill. Typically your novel will be dissected by a copy editor. Copy editors are a specialized form of editor. Their main task is to assure your novel is grammatically correct, formatted correctly, stylistically reliable, and has no consistency problems. For example, if a side character's name was Teddy in Chapter Two and you only refer to that character as Theodore in the last couple chapters of the book, you will be asked to make this consistent. Another consistency problem might be that your character answered the phone or the door without mention of any ring or knock, or that the hero's house faced south in Chapter One but east in Chapter Seven.

The important thing to know about copy editors is that you're not obliged to take their suggested changes. Copy editors are people, too. You might have an illiterate, homeless, unbalanced individual talking in ungrammatical gibberish, which the copy editor might correct to the Queen's English. Pay attention to their suggestions, but don't forget that you're the writer. This is your novel. Keep it the way you wrote it when there's a reason for doing so.

It's possible the editor may have changes of her own. If so, the same guidelines apply as with a copy editor. The difference is that you consider the editor's suggestions with extra care and you should be prepared to defend (argue for) your position on any suggestions you reject.

Marketing

Your publishing house might ask you to schedule book signings, interviews, and other marketing opportunities.

Provided you even have access to any physical bookstores, I suggest keeping book signings to a minimum. They take a great deal of time/energy and produce negligible results.

This will be covered more in the next part of this book, but I would suggest you concentrate your marketing efforts on techniques that provide the most bang for the buck. While I'd never hesitate to sell your novel one-on-one to someone you happen to meet, you're not going to garner many readers this way.

The best way to increase the sales for your novel is through mass media, including advertising. That means television, radio, newspaper, and internet. The underlying principle is that you want one marketing effort to reach as many readers as possible.

Beyond that, for a traditionally published novel, your main technique for creating sales is to write and publish awesome books at a phenomenal rate and allow your readership to grow by word-of-mouth.

There is too much. Let me sum up

Getting published typically means playing by industry rules and following industry standards that have remained relatively unchanged for decades.

- Editors and agents evaluate your manuscript differently than people who read for pleasure.
- At a minimum, most first-novels have a great beginning and a great ending.
- Editors and agents often reject incoming manuscripts using shortcuts that allow them to quickly evaluate the likelihood that a manuscript should be published.
- Unless you want to wait years for your novel to be accepted (or rejected), you either need to know an editor personally or get yourself an agent (or get win-the-lottery lucky).
- Research agents carefully and query ones most likely to represent your work.
- A query letter is a business letter that represents you and your book in its best light and whose sole purpose is to interest the agent and convince them to request a synopsis.
- If a query letter is a 30-second ad for your novel, your synopsis is equivalent to an infomercial for your book.
- A book proposal is a combination of your cover letter, your synopsis, and sample chapters.
- Never surrender all rights to anything unless those rights weren't yours to begin with (such as with a media tie-in novel or a work-for-hire situation).

- Before signing any contract, make sure you understand, accept, and are prepared to satisfy any terms specified by the contract.
- Any marketing efforts you make on behalf of your novel should concentrate on mass media outlets where you can reach the most readers with the least time and effort.

Part III: Marketing

Not My Job

I wish someone else had written this book and I had read it before Tor published my first novel. Even though I'd been in the business long enough to know that traditional publishers barely lift a finger to promote a novel by a new author and that most of the marketing was up to me, I didn't know how to market my novel. Even so, I didn't stand on the sideline doing nothing. I managed to snag articles in several newspapers, did four book signings, and one radio interview. I created a web site devoted to the release of the novel. I created marketing materials and distributed them in any place that made any sense at all.

And it meant nothing.

The reason was simple. It just wasn't enough. I didn't understand that marketing my novel required nearly as much effort and time as writing it. More important, doing 90% of the marketing required to sell a novel isn't much different than doing 10%. Until you reach a critical threshold of readers that allows your novel to start selling through word of mouth, you really have no chance.

Fortunately, in today's world, marketing is easier than ever before. It still takes times, but using the techniques covered on the following pages, it's possible to effectively market a first novel and make a real impact on sales.

"Wait!" you scream. "That's why I sold my novel to traditional publishers in the first place—so that I wouldn't need to do all this marketing stuff!"

Forgive me while I shake my head and tsk-tsk sadly.

When it comes to marketing, it doesn't matter whether your book is being published by one of the big five out of New York or whether you're publishing it yourself. Unless you received a six-figure advance, the amount of marketing you will receive will do nothing to sell your book. Even if this isn't the case, do you really want to take that chance? You wrote your novel so that people could read it. They can't read it if they don't know it exists.

If you want to be a successful writer, you better learn to be a successful marketer.

The Fine Print

Many of the techniques I cover are directed at writers who are just starting out. It's easy to market your work when you have a large body of work to market and a loyal following of devoted readers. What I'm more concerned with in this chapter is marketing your first novel or your first couple of novels. Having said that, plenty of the techniques covered here will serve you well throughout your writing career. Adjust my advice as needed to fit your current situation.

Brand I Am

People love brands they can trust. In our modern world, buying decisions are more complicated than ever before. If you can find a brand that delivers, your buying decision becomes easy: Just look for that brand.

For writers, this concept of brand is not limited simply to name alone. Sure, if you're an avid reader who loves Stephen King or Dean Koontz, you buy a novel simply because it's written by one of those writers. But what about J. K. Rowling? She has plenty of brand clout, too, but her personal author brand pales in comparison to the Harry Potter brand. When I talk to people about their favorite novels, I hear plenty of readers who say they love Harry Potter. Few say they love J. K. Rowling. It's not that they don't love J. K. Rowling—they do—but when they think of her, they think of Harry Potter first.

As authors, when we talk about branding, we have two considerations. If you're a writer of stand-alone novels, you're marketing your own name. If you write series, you're marketing both the series name and your own name. After all, you'll probably finish that series someday and you'd love your readers to join you on your next great adventure.

What you want are satisfied readers who trust your brand. Violate that trust and you risk losing that reader forever.

Who Am I Today?

Most readers like certain kinds (genres) of novels more than others. You don't want the fans of your hard-boiled police procedural series making the mistake of picking up your latest young adult romance novel expecting to find a police procedural. Some writers think this situation is fine—it's another book sold—but sell a book and lose a reader forever is not a good tradeoff.

Using pseudonyms to distinguish between novels written in different genres isn't always necessary, but it's a time-honored technique used by writers for decades. Research shows that midlist and below writers receive few crossover buys between the various genres they write. While releasing all of your novels under your own name has a certain appeal, it's hard to justify from a marketing standpoint if you write novels in widely differing genres. If you write a subsequent novel in a genre where no one knows you, don't be surprised if your agent or editor asks you to adopt a pseudonym for all the books you write in that genre.

Talk Once, Sell Many Times

I know hundreds of writers who think a great marketing plan consists of doing signings, composing a blog, interacting with people on social media, and otherwise building their readers one at a time. The problem with this concept is that it's not efficient. For every hour you commit to marketing, you have one less hour to write. While every devoted and admiring reader is precious, there is a better way to gain those readers.

The bulk of your marketing time and dollars should focus on doing the marketing once and having the chance at many readers in return. Part of this is getting the word out to places and people who are likely to spread the word further still. Here are a few examples of this work once, get many readers philosophy:

- Television, radio, and newspaper interviews
- Book reviews
- Advertising
- Web Site and author pages
- Newsletter

All of these techniques involve very different skills. As such, we should probably take them one at a time and see what we can make of them.

Television, Radio, and Newspaper Interviews

Entry into any of these outlets is typically an uphill battle. Lots of people have something to sell. What you must have is something to offer as well as something to sell. While successful self-promotion through the media is a topic worthy of a book unto itself (or perhaps a series of books), a few general pieces of advice are handy:

1) Learn how to write a press release. An easy way to do this is to google "how to write a press release." It's a learned skill, which means it's a skill *you* can *learn*.
2) Figure out a way to leverage any knowledge or background material that went into your novel. Likely targets are science, history, and geography. This is one advantage provided by writing about real places rather than made-up towns and cities.
3) Learn how to give a good interview and remember that while your eventual goal is the promotion of your novel, your immediate task with everything you say is to be entertaining.

Don't get discouraged if your first attempts to land an interview fail. Also, no interview is too small, especially when you're starting out. That interview for the local paper gives you valuable practice for later in life when you're being interviewed for an audience of millions. If you don't prepare for it to happen, it never will.

Book Reviews

The person reviewing your book is more important than the review itself. Does that person have a following? If so, what kind of following? You want reviews from people who mainly read novels like the one you wrote. If their focus is narrow, the chance of their review being viewed by others who would want to buy your book goes up. So, if you want the "right" people to review your book, start by looking at who reviewed recently-released books that are similar to yours and send your book to those people for review.

Beyond that, try not to pay too much attention to reviews of your book. Whether a particular reader liked or didn't like your novel is irrelevant. The only helpful information you can gain is why a reader felt the way they did. Were they the wrong type of reader? If so, then their negative (or positive) review says more about them (or more about your advertising and marketing) than it does your work. Learn from your reviews and move on. It's guaranteed people exist who will hate your book no matter how good the book is. If you have no negative reviews, you simply haven't found those people yet.

Only pay attention to positive or negative reviews when the reviewer is kind enough to say what they liked (or didn't like) about your novel. For example, if you introduced a new character in the third book of your series and that character receives mention in multiple reviews, then that information is pure gold. Do the readers like the new character? Do they hate him? Do they like him in general but hate his political views? While you can't bend your series to the opinions of your readers, it's just good business sense to nudge the series toward the likes and away from the dislikes of your readers. Either that, or adjust your marketing so that you're not targeting people who aren't going to like your book no matter how well it's written.

Advertising

It'd be great if I could tell you exactly what you need to do to advertise your novel effectively. Unfortunately, every book is different just as every writer is different. As with reviews, you want to target your advertising toward people who have a good chance to like your novel. Advertising across the board is so ineffective that it's useless.

Opportunities for advertising your novel change almost daily. To decide if an advertising opportunity is right for you, evaluate it on the following criteria:

1) How well does it target the readers you want versus readers in general?
2) How much does it cost per response?
3) How well can you measure your success?

In a perfect world, your advertising will reach only the readers you're interested in reaching, will cost a fraction of what you make per sale, and will provide every useful metric you can imagine. In reality, one or more of these areas will be less than you would prefer, but they provide a useful measuring stick for effectiveness.

Since advertising is so complex, I've covered what you need to know in much more detail under "The World's Oldest Profession" section.

Web Site and Author Pages

Having your own web site is important, because it's the only internet based web site over which you have complete control. Ultimate power has its uses. Plus the cost of having your own web site is minimal for a professional author. If the revenue from your writing doesn't provide enough funds to support your own web site, then you're still in the wanna-be writer, hobby phase of your career. There's nothing wrong with that, but you have to invest in yourself at some point. Creating your own web site is as good a place to start as any.

Many services provide free pages for authors to use for promoting their work. Some common examples are the author page on Amazon, a celebrity Facebook page, and the author page on Goodreads. Many others exist. While it can be time-consuming to get all of these set up with relevant and intriguing information including the image of your smiling mug, the update rate of these pages can be minimal. Some helpful guidelines:

1) All public displays should be as professional and as well thought out as you have time to make them.
2) Update these pages regularly, but don't overwhelm your followers.

Along with web pages spreading the good word, feel free to utilize Twitter and any other electronic communication service that allows you to reach your readers. The warning I give here is that using a service like Twitter for self-promotion alone is like working at a restaurant for 8 hours every day because you're hungry. Sure, you're surrounded by food, but it takes you forever to get anything to eat. Said another way, feel free to use these frequent update services if you're already using them. If not, they're probably not worth the time they'll steal from your writing.

Newsletter

For most authors, your newsletter should be nothing more than a quick chat with your readers to announce something *related to your work* that they would find relevant. You can certainly do more than this, but the length and frequency of your newsletter relates directly to how useful and entertaining your readers find your newsletters to be. I know writers who can hit their readers with a newsletter every day. The readers eat it up because the writer is such a dynamic personality or shares such fascinating information that the readers simply can't get enough. For other writers, each time they send out a newsletter, they risk losing readers. Know your strengths and your weaknesses. Lean on your newsletter accordingly.

Besides deciding what to put in your newsletter and deciding how often to send it, you need to know who to send it to. The answer to this question is quite simple, even if making it happen can be time-consuming and difficult. Only send your newsletter to people who are likely to enjoy whatever book you're telling them about. This means that you don't want everyone on the planet reading your newsletter. Newsletters (and the lists of readers those newsletters are sent to) provide an invaluable resource for each new book you release. No advertising in existence beats telling people who are interested in a product that such a product is available and telling them where they can get one of their very own.

The reasons you want to restrict the readers on your list only to those who would be interested in what you have to sell them is because this allows you to evaluate the success or failure of any announcement. Plus, it gives you a loyal band of followers who provide information you simply can't get anywhere else. Thinking of ending your series at book 10? Let your newsletter readers know and see what kind of reaction you get. Thinking of writing a new series that might interest these readers? Drop a line about your new possible project and see what the response is.

Reader Magnets

The Catch-22 of newsletters is that getting people to sign up for one works best after those people are already fans of your writing. So how do you start out? For writing nonfiction, it's pretty easy. Make snippets of information available related to your subject with the promise of more complete and detailed information available in newsletter form. Then when your nonfiction book is released, you already have a following of people who are naturally interested in your book. But what about fiction? How do you attract readers before you have any readers?

In simple terms, you have to have already written something. I know some writers who've done this by giving away short stories that would be interesting to the same readers who would enjoy their novels. That typically means the same characters and the same genre. At the end of each short story, you put in a link that takes readers to a page where they can sign up for your newsletter. As an alternative, you can request your publisher to add links to your web page to the back material of your novel. Granted, this doesn't help you sell that novel, but it does start the email list building process that should benefit you down the road. Many writers offer their readers something for free if they sign up for their newsletter, but when you're just starting out, be wary of giving away everything you've written to date. If your novel is good enough, your readers will want to know when the next novel in the series is being released. If your novel isn't good enough, you've already lost the battle, so offering trinkets in exchange for their email addresses doesn't provide you with much.

The great thing about reader magnets is that you have full control over the magnets themselves, the resulting list of emails, and the newsletter.

There are multiple web sites that allow you to force readers to sign up for your newsletter in order to be allowed to download your freebie short story. An important consideration with any giveaway that requires readers to sign up for your newsletter is that you're attracting exactly the wrong sort of crowd. What I mean by that is: You're attracting people who are looking for something free to read. Later, you try to sell them books. See the conflict? On the other hand, if you put a join-my-newsletter link in the back of the first novel in your series or the back of a freely published short story, you've guaranteed that those readers made it to the back of your book or story before they signed up. Generally this means they read what you wrote. If they sign up at that point, it means they like what you've written and are interested in the next installment. You'll sign up a lot less total people this way, but the readers you have will be more likely to buy than a bunch of freebie hunters.

Quality leads on your newsletter list are much more valuable than people who will delete your emails without opening them.

What about a Blog?

Some authors write more in their blogs than they do their books. For nonfiction authors, blogs can be an effective marketing tool. For fiction writers, blogs provide uncertain benefits at best. It's not hard to imagine a group of readers who love a writer's blog but don't care much for his fiction; yet, they still buy his books out of loyalty. It may seem like any reader is a good reader to have, but in our modern world, this is definitely not true.

Blogs work best for fiction writers when a nonfiction subject overlaps nicely with fiction interests. For example, many hard science-fiction authors are interested in space exploration. If you're a sf author who blogs about the latest space missions and rocket technology being developed, chances are good that a significant block of your readers would be interested in your latest space opera novel. If you're a romance writer who blogs about ways to improve your marital relationship, chances are good many of your blog readers are the same readers buying your novels.

Two main problems keep blogs from being an effective marketing tool when you're first starting out: 1) Time spent getting people to follow your blog could be spent getting people to buy your books, and 2) Blogs are a clumsy and inaccurate tool for reaching your fiction readers. A newsletter directed at readers who want to know when your next book is coming out is much more effective and much less time consuming. Just as with social media such as Twitter and Pinterest, if you're already writing a blog, keep writing it. If you're not writing one yet, there are probably better ways to spend your marketing time.

The World's Oldest Profession

According to Wikipedia, Rudyard Kipling is widely credited with associating the world's oldest profession with prostitution. But Kipling had it wrong. Before any money, goods, or services ever changed hands, somebody had to sell somebody else on the idea of giving up something they wanted for something they wanted more. I would argue then that sales is the world's oldest profession. For writer's, we're selling our books, which often feels like we're selling a piece of ourselves. While we can do that by marching down the street, banging a drum, and yelling, "Buy my books!" it isn't a particularly effective use of our time.

A better way to sell our wares is by using the same method nearly everyone else does: advertising. Notice that I didn't say "a profitable way." While many writers make advertising a cash-in activity, there are no guarantees. Like everything associated with writing, the more skilled you are, the more likely you are to succeed.

Nail the Freebies

The most effective (and most important) forms of advertising writers have available are ones over which you have little to no control as a traditionally published novelist:

- Cover
- Title
- Tagline
- Blurb

Fortunately, one of the advantages of traditional publishing is that these free marketing materials are created professionals who do this for a living. That doesn't guarantee success, but typically it does mean you receive professional quality.

Most publishers I've worked with ask you to come up with ideas (or full creations) for some or all of these. They are least likely to request or respect your opinions regarding the cover, but often the other three items are influenced if not totally controlled by your input. As such, I've covered each of these items individually.

Cover

If your cover doesn't hook your readers, everything else you might do to market the book pales in comparison. All readers judge books by their covers first, even if they don't realize it. In today's information-overdriven world, covers that don't get noticed don't get seen. But getting seen isn't enough. If you manage to attract a reader's eye, you need to convince that eye to linger long enough for its owner to consider your book. So much goes into this nearly instantaneous judgment that no one understands exactly what differentiates a successful cover from one that's merely passable, but there are some criteria you can evaluate, some of which are more black and white than others:

- Your cover needs to look great both as a full-size image and as a thumbnail.
- The book's title should be easily readable on the thumbnail image.
- The overall look, color, and font on the cover should match currently-selling novels in your book's genre.
- Have extra space between the letters of your name and between the letters in the title, meaning each letter is further apart than normal text in a book, like this for example.

- Seek a cover as pleasing to the eye as possible, meaning it's both pleasant and interesting to look at.
- Urge simplicity. In general, simpler covers outsell more complex covers.
- The cover should "pop," meaning it has significant contrast between some of the elements.

What you can't allow is a misrepresentation of your novel. They say you catch more flies with honey than with vinegar. Your honey is a cover that attracts readers who are most likely to want to buy what you're selling. Your vinegar is a cover that your desired readers don't associate with books they like to read. If your cover looks great but makes your sf novel look like it's a horror novel, you're not going to attract the science fiction readers you actually wanted. Worse yet, if those horror readers happen to buy your novel and read it, they're probably not going to like it.

Make sure your cover matches your genre.

While your publishing house is going to be least likely to listen to your thoughts regarding your cover, don't hesitate to make the attempt. Just because you'll be getting a professional cover, it doesn't mean that particular cover is a good fit for your novel. Do the research yourself. Request changes if your initial cover isn't right. Just remember that cover is a marketing tool first and a cool picture second.

Title

While titles don't have the same importance as covers or even blurbs and taglines, they should still attract the right kind of reader. The best titles perform triple duty: They're interesting, they convey the genre perfectly, and they catch one or more common search keywords while still being unique. For example, police procedural mysteries might have titles like: *Dead Stop, Her Last Goodbye,* or *The Deepest Grave.* Regency romances might have titles like: *Loving a Noble Gentleman, Amelia and the Viscount,* or *A Governess for the Brooding Duke.*

While some writers will put more emphasis on titles than is necessary, your title is how most word-of-mouth recommendations happen, at least until you become famous. That means you want your book's title to be relatively easy to remember. You also want your series titles to be relatively easy to remember. While titles can't be copyrighted, it's still best to google your title and make sure your book won't get confused with someone else's.

From a practical standpoint, the length of the title comes into play, especially in today's world of shopping via thumbnail. The longer your title, the harder it is to fit on the cover at a size large enough to be readable.

Of the four free marketing tools mentioned in this section, your title is the one element you'll likely be able to control. Make sure you get it right.

Tagline

Your tagline may never appear on the cover of your novel or in any of the marketing materials created by your publishing house. However, there's an excellent chance you created a tagline for your cover letter or your synopsis. You may have even met with and spoken to your editor personally and used your tagline to sell the book. As such, your tagline is often used to market your book to your agent and editor.

Taglines are the shortest way for you to tell a prospective agent or editor just enough about your book to convince them they want to know more. Typically taglines are one sentence long. If each sentence is just a few words, multiple sentences work. For example, the horror movie Willard was based on a novel called *Ratman's Notebooks*. If we were to write a tagline for that novel, we might say:

> A lonely boy. A pack of rats. Sweet revenge.

I'm not saying it's great (Stephen Gilbert's estate isn't paying me to write taglines for his old novel), but it conveys the point. It's horrifying for most people. A boy. Rats. Revenge? It certainly doesn't sound pleasant, which is exactly what we're looking for. This is a dark novel and the tagline should attract readers who are interested in that type of story.

While I know many writers who've sold a ton of books without ever writing a single tagline, you never know when your tagline might be used on your cover rather than one generated by the house's marketing department.

A further benefit of taglines is that they can be used for paid advertising. A great tagline never goes to waste.

Blurb

Next to your cover, your blurb is the one over which you often have the least control. Regardless, all the publishing houses I've dealt with based their back cover blurb as well as the book's description in their catalog on information I supplied. This means that you should know how to write a good blurb for your novel.

The job of your blurb is simple: Convince any potential reader that this is a book that they would like to read, provided they're a reader who really would like to read it. While sales of any kind are nice in the short-term, devoted readers who actually like what you've written are much more important to long-term success. This will become clearer as we go through advertising options, but it's not hard to understand that if more people read all your books instead of just your first book, selling that first book becomes much more valuable.

This is where research comes into play. Every genre is different. You want to appeal to people who will like the type of book you've written. Figure out what books your book resembles and then examine the blurbs created for those books.

Spend Money to Make Money

As a new writer without a six-figure deal or some extra attention from your house, chances of earning back your advance without significant marketing effort from you is minimal. Also, as a traditionally published writer, you're working on a pass-fail system. Sell too few copies and you won't be selling any future novels to your house (and probably not to any others). While it's impossible to know how many copies you need to sell to make your publisher happy, you're fairly safe if you earn back your advance.

What do I mean by earn back your advance?

The real answer to this question is beyond the scope of this book. Profitability on any given title is extremely complex, but for simplicity's sake, we'll use the meaning that most authors use: Earning back your advance means that the publisher sold enough books to have paid you your advance using the royalties for the books that sold. For example, if you make $1 per book in royalties and your advance was $3,000, the publisher would need to sell 3,000 books (after subtracting returns) before you had "earned back your advance."

As a traditionally published author, you certainly hope that your house will do enough marketing to sell some of your books without your direct help. The rest will need to be marketed by you. While it's extremely unlikely you'll make enough in royalties per book sold to pay for the advertising you need to sell that book, you need to determine how much your future writing career is worth. Certainly you should avail yourself of the marketing opportunities covered by "Talk Once, Sell Many Times," but unless you excel at those, you'll need some extra help.

Decide how much you want to spend on advertising and then try to use that investment as efficiently as possible. At the very least, create an Amazon ad when your book is released. Put in a bid of $0.20 per click or lower. You can also set a daily spending limit on Amazon, but chances are you'll never reach it. After a month, you might have only spent $20 or $30. If you're doing everything else you can to market your book, assume the ad is working and let it go.

You can spend half your working day analyzing and tweaking the various forms of advertising you're using to sell your books. Or you could write another couple novels with all those hours. We all have different levels of interest in marketing. If it's something you enjoy, get into it as far as you want. If you hate the very idea, learn enough so that you don't cost yourself a small fortune if you make a mistake.

Pay to Play

The only paid advertising I'll examine from this point on is on-line advertising. While it's perfectly feasible to advertise using billboards, newspapers and magazines, book video trailers, radio and television commercials, and direct mail flyers, the price point for effective entry into any of those advertising mediums is a couple of orders of magnitude higher than it is with on-line advertising. As such, it's much riskier. Most authors who aren't independently wealthy therefore avoid laying out that kind of cash with no promise of return.

As for the on-line advertising market, we'll restrict our discussion to the two used most often by writers I know. These two paid advertising mediums have worked (and worked wildly) for many authors:

- Amazon Ads
- Facebook Ads

I've covered each of these mediums in the sections below.

<u>Amazon Ads</u>

The single greatest advantage of buying ads through Amazon is that those ads go straight to people who buy books at Amazon. More important, those ads go to people precisely when they're shopping for books on Amazon. This is gold. It's like the impulse items next to the checkout in a grocery store. Your potential readers are buying books. Hey, here's your book! Why not buy it?

While this is pretty wonderful stuff, it's hard to overestimate the advantage provided by marketing your novel to an audience that's likely to be interested in buying and is already on the site (or in the app) that allows them to make the purchase immediately.

Amazon ads work.

That is, they work if you've got a great cover, title, tagline, and blurb—and you've written a decent book. Also, you need to select a good set of keywords for your Sponsored Products ads and the correct Targeted Interests for your Product Display Ads. There are plenty of specialized books available that will cover exactly how to do Amazon Ads, such as *Mastering Amazon Ads* by Brian D. Meeks.

Amazon ads aren't perfect. Like all advertising, they don't come with a guarantee of success. Also, Amazon customers are getting fairly jaded against the ads. Many Amazon customers have trained themselves to look at the Also-Boughts but ignore the Sponsored Products. You can get around this by using Product Display Ads by Interest. Those type of ads are sometimes displayed as a person's Kindle screensaver, which means they have sole possession of a reader's interest, however briefly. Also, Amazon ads tend to die after a time. They simply quit working.

For me, this highlights the biggest problem with Amazon ads, which is also a problem with Facebook ads. To work best, they require constant maintenance. Granted, I know authors who start up a single Amazon ad and have it run effectively for months without ever touching it. I know many others who try ten different ads and only get one to work.

The biggest caution I will give is that the effectiveness of Amazon ads changes constantly. Do a bit of research before starting your own sets of Amazon ads.

As far as judging the results of your Amazon ads, here are some handy targets you should be trying to hit:

- Average Cost Per Click (ACPC) should be less than 20¢
- Clicks Per 1,000 Impressions should be 1 or higher

- Average Clicks Per Sale should be between 5 and 20 with a reasonable goal of 10

f you hit the ACPS goal, you're going to spend $1.50-2.00 for every book you sell. Certainly I know a lot of writers who do much better than this with their ads, but most of them devote a lot of time to tweaking, creating, and maintaining those ads.

Getting a click every 1,000 impressions tells you if your ad is working. Plus, Amazon tends to limit ads (not show them much) for any ads that get less than one click per 1,000 impressions.

Having those clicks cost less than 20¢ each just means you have a better chance that you'll make a profit on the ads. Also, there doesn't seem to be any relationship between paying more for your ad and getting any additional sales. Why pay more for less?

If your results don't match the targets I provided above, the ones that are off give you a clue as to what you need to change. If your average cost per click is too high, lower the amount of your bids. If your clicks to impressions ratio is too low, improve your ad blurb and re-examine your keywords.

One of the benefits of Amazon (and Facebook) ads is that you know whether potential readers have viewed your book listing on Amazon. Granted, sometimes folks will accidentally click where they didn't mean to click, but nearly all of the clicks you see on your ad results represent readers who thought your ad thumbnail and copy were interesting enough that they wanted to find out more. If you're getting a ton of clicks and not selling, either you're attracting the wrong type of readers or your cover/tagline/

blurb need improvement. Unfortunately, those aren't under your control.

Facebook Ads

In my experience, Facebook ads are more expensive and result in fewer sales per click. So why use them? Mainly because the folks at Amazon Marketing Services are really slow on the uptake in some ways. They may get there eventually, but right now Amazon provides almost no analytics. As a result, you have almost no data related to any Amazon ad beyond the basics of impressions, clicks, and average cost-per-click. Eventually (usually days later) you get information about any sales you may have made.

In comparison, Facebook gives you so many ways to analyze your ad results, you might need a degree in Advertising to take advantage of all the possibilities. For simple writer folks like me, some of the most useful information beyond the basics are the results based on age and gender as well as time of day. How much of this information you want to look at is up to you, but the point is that you can look at it. Facebook makes it available to you.

In addition, there are millions of ways to configure the audience who sees your Facebook ad. You can target by interest, behavior, age, etc. You can save audiences once you get them just right or you can change the audience for an ad after it's ran a few days or weeks. This is great. It's not as good as Amazon ads that automatically target folks while they're in book-buying mode, but it still gives you a great deal of control.

If you want to learn a ton about Facebook ads from someone who's made them work for years, I'd recommend

Michael Cooper's *Help! My Facebook Ads Suck*. The details of these advertising possibilities are more than worthy of an entire book. Here we're covering what you need to know, but if you want to know more, there are resources available.

In order to judge the results of your Facebook ads (like we did for our Amazon ads), here are some handy targets you should be trying to hit:

- Average Cost Per Click (ACPC) should be less than 30¢
- Relevancy score of at least 8
- Frequency as close to 1 as you can keep it
- Average Clicks Per Sale should be between 20 and 40 with a reasonable goal of 30

The first thing you should notice about these targets is that they're not nearly as optimistic as the Amazon ad targets. That's because Facebook ads don't work as efficiently as Amazon ads. The people who love Facebook ads might argue, but the simple truth is that it's much harder to sell someone a book when they're not book shopping than it is to sell someone a book when they are book shopping. If everything else is equal, that means it will cost you more per sale using Facebook ads than it will using Amazon ads.

Once again, this begs the question: Why use Facebook ads instead of Amazon ads?

The answer is two-fold: Facebook has millions of users and Facebook will spend your money. The biggest problem advertising on Amazon results from Amazon's limited advertising space. This lack of ad inundation makes the ads that are there more effective, but it means you can give Amazon a daily budget of $10 and Amazon may only spend 50¢ of that. You might be selling a book for every

$1 you spend on Amazon, but it takes you two days to sell one book. Some people claim to know how to scale up their advertising on Amazon, but I've seen way more failure stories than success stories for folks who have tried.

If you give Facebook $10 per day to spend, they'll typically spend the whole $10, at least until you've saturated your market. As a traditionally published author, you have a limited amount of time to earn back your advance before your publishing house writes your novel off as a bad job. For most writers, there's just no way to spend enough on Amazon to sell the number of books you need to sell in the time available to you. That's why Facebook shines and Amazon comes up short.

Speaking of saturating your market, that brings us to Frequency. That's the number Facebook attaches to your results to let you know how many times each person has seen your ad. Facebook doesn't want to repeat the same ads to the same users, because they discovered folks don't like that. As a result, as your Frequency score climbs, your Relevancy score falls. However, if you have an ad that's working great (has a Relevancy score of 10 with low ACPC and great sales results), there's no harm in letting your Frequency number climb as the ad runs its course. That's why you can ignore the Frequency if you wish and just pay attention to the Relevancy score, which Facebook starts to calculate after 500 impressions or so.

Relevancy is based on multiple factors. In simple terms, if enough people who are shown your ad are interested in your ad, your Relevancy score will be high. If less people are interested, your Relevancy score will be lower. One important note on all of the Facebook ad targets mentioned above: Don't pay attention to any of them until you get t least 500 impressions and obtain that Relevancy score. This is because ads can start off ridiculously high, get a Relevancy score of 10, and perform fantastic afterwards.

Following are some general guidelines about how to construct effective Facebook ads.

People on Facebook aren't shopping, so don't have your ad look like an ad. This means your ad should look more like a normal Facebook post and less like an ad. To do this, use a good picture that does *not* contain text. This means that you should not use the cover of your book. Typically you should also not use part of the cover of your book unless it's a really great picture and doesn't really look like a book cover. This is because Facebook doesn't serve ads that contain text in the picture to nearly as many people while simultaneously charging way more for the people who do respond to the ad. While it's true that Facebook ads with text-containing pictures are allowed as long as they're part of a book cover, those ads never perform as well as Facebook ads with pictures that don't contain text.

Have all the links in your ad point to your page on Amazon. You typically run Facebook ads to sell your book. Using them for anything else is prohibitively expensive compared to other methods of advertising.

Also consider getting another Amazon account and use it as your Amazon Affiliate account. Then use a different Affiliate tag for each ad. This changes your Click-Through data into sales data. Note that Amazon says this is prohibited. If they discover you're doing it, they'll shut down your Affiliate account, but it's the only current way to track sales results on Amazon from non-Amazon ads until Amazon wises up and provides us with a way to do that.

Which Way Do I Go?

These two online advertising methods aren't exclusive. Most authors I know use both as well as others we didn't cover. Readers can be reached in many different ways. If you find an advertising medium that lets you reach readers at a reasonable cost and doesn't suck up your entire life to make it work, it's usually worth the effort.

There is too much. Let me sum up

Marketing is important to all writers at every stage of their careers. No matter how successful you are, you can increase your success through marketing, if you do it well.

- The main branding control all authors maintain is the author name they attach to their novels. The easiest way to help your readers distinguish between the different types (genres) of books you write is by using a pseudonym unique to each.
- The most efficient type of marketing an author can do always involves reaching the greatest number of potential readers for each marketing action taken. For example, being interviewed for any public media format is always more effective than doing a book-signing.
- Use as many types of marketing as you can to get the word out to your readers, including doing interviews and press releases, having a web page, sending a newsletter to readers of your previous work, encouraging book reviews, and employing advertising targeted toward likely readers.
- Your cover should look great as a full image and a thumbnail, should pop with at least one area of contrast, have easy-to-read and pleasing fonts, and should have a readable title, even when viewed as a thumbnail.
- Having an interesting tagline serves multiple purposes and is always useful.

- Amazon ads tend to be the most efficient, common, on-line ads but they're difficult to scale and degrade over time.
- Facebook ads are easier to scale but are less efficient and tend to cost more than Amazon ads per sale

A Final Word

Nothing is more thrilling than getting that acceptance letter, email, or phone call for your first published novel. To do that, your manuscript should be the best you can possibly make it and should be written as quickly as you can while keeping your quality as high as it can be.

To help you do just that, please consider the other books in the Write a Great Novel series:

- *Writing Quickly While Writing Well*
- *Story and Characters*
- *Beginning to End*

If you'd prefer, you can get all the books from the Write a Great Novel series compiled into one handy volume (which will always be less expensive than buying the books individually):

- *Write a Great Novel: The Wonderful Writing Secrets of Oz*

If you have any writing-related questions, don't hesitate to contact me by leaving a comment on my Facebook page:

http://www.facebook.com/grsixbury/

Index

D

E

F

G

H

I

J

K

www.ingramcontent.com/pod-product-compliance
Lightning Source LLC
Chambersburg PA
CBHW022116280326
41933CB00007B/417